Holly-Jolly CRAFTS UNDER $10

*W*ant to stretch your Christmas cash? Then you've come to the right source: the crafting experts of Leisure Arts. This book has more than 80 clever new ideas to make your holidays merry — and every one can be made for under $10, and often for even less than $5! You'll be amazed at how thrifty it is to make crafts that are oh-so-nifty, using ordinary, inexpensive materials that you probably have in your home right now! From festive wreaths and ornaments to fun clothing and photo albums, your creations will sparkle with professional quality, yet glow with the warmth and charm that come from being handmade. For every project, you'll have our simple-to-follow instructions, complete materials lists, and a cost breakdown of how much you can expect to spend. It's okay to beam with pride when folks say "I can't believe you made this just for me!" But don't tell anyone how easy and inexpensive they were to make — that's our little secret!

Anne Childs

LEISURE ARTS, INC.
Little Rock, Arkansas

Holly-Jolly CRAFTS UNDER $10

EDITORIAL STAFF

Vice President and Editor-in-Chief: Anne Van Wagner Childs
Executive Director: Sandra Graham Case
Design Director: Patricia Wallenfang Sowers
Editorial Director: Susan Frantz Wiles
Publications Director: Kristine Anderson Mertes
Creative Art Director: Gloria Bearden

DESIGN
Designers: Polly Tullis Browning, Diana Sanders Cates, Cherece Athy Cooper, Cyndi Hansen, Dani Martin, Sandra Spots Ritchie, Billie Steward, Anne Pulliam Stocks, and Linda Diehl Tiano
Executive Assistant: Debra Smith
Design Assistants: Diana Sanders Cates, Dani Martin, and Melanie Vaughan

TECHNICAL
Managing Editor: Sherry Solida Ford
Senior Technical Writers: Laura Lee Powell and Kimberly J. Smith
Technical Writers: Jennifer Potts Hutchings, Susan McManus Johnson, Marley N. Washum, and Theresa Hicks Young
Technical Associates: Susan Frazier, Linda Luder, and Candice Treat Murphy

EDITORIAL
Managing Editor: Linda L. Trimble
Coordinating Editor: Terri Leming Davidson
Associate Editors: Stacey Robertson Marshall and Janice Teipen Wojcik

ART
Book/Magazine Graphic Art Director: Diane Thomas
Graphic Artist and Color Technician: Mark Hawkins
Photography Stylists: Beth Carter, Ellen J. Clifton, Sondra Daniel, Karen Smart Hall, Kim Hocott, and Aurora Huston
Publishing Systems Administrator: Cynthia M. Lumpkin
Publishing Systems Assistant: Myra S. Means

PROMOTIONS
Managing Editor: Alan Caudle
Associate Editor: Steven M. Cooper
Designer: Dale Rowett
Art Director: Linda Lovette Smart

BUSINESS STAFF

Publisher: Rick Barton
Vice President and General Manager: Thomas L. Carlisle
Vice President, Finance: Tom Siebenmorgen
Vice President, Retail Marketing: Bob Humphrey
Vice President, National Accounts: Pam Stebbins

Retail Marketing Director: Margaret Sweetin
General Merchandise Manager: Cathy Laird
Distribution Director: Rob Thieme
Retail Customer Service Manager: Wanda Price
Print Production Manager: Fred F. Pruss

Library of Congress Catalog Number 99-71588
International Standard Book Number 1-57486-125-5

10 9 8 7 6 5 4 3 2 1

Table of Contents

Table of Contents

Table of Contents

Make an ENTRANCE

*L*et your front door extend
a merry welcome to everyone
who comes to visit during the
holidays! Whatever your style —
naturally charming, gleaming with
elegance, simply rustic, or brightly
whimsical — we've got the perfect
door decor just for you. And best
of all, you won't have to spend
a fortune like your neighbors
probably did! Just turn the page
and let us show you how to make
a truly impressive entrance.

7

NATURAL APPEAL

*P*inecones, dried flowers, and jute twine lend rustic appeal to our evergreen wreath. Homestyle touches include padded paper-bag gingerbread men and fabric-wrapped foam balls. It's a real country charmer!

WHAT TO BUY

24" dia. artificial evergreen wreath, six 2" dia. plastic foam balls, 1/4 yd. of cotton batting, and dried German statice

THINGS YOU HAVE AT HOME

Scraps of assorted fabrics, straight pins, tracing paper, brown paper bags, pinking shears, craft glue, paper-backed fusible web, buttons, black permanent fine-point pen, pinecones, jute twine, and a hot glue gun

RUSTIC HOLIDAY WREATH

1. For each ball ornament, tear six 1" x 9" strips of fabric. Overlapping long edges and twisting fabric at bottom of foam ball, wrap strips around ball; secure with straight pins.

2. Trace pattern, page 116, onto tracing paper; cut out. For each gingerbread man ornament, draw around pattern twice on brown paper and once on batting. Cut out batting shape. Use pinking shears to cut out paper shapes slightly inside drawn line. Positioning batting shape between paper shapes, use craft glue to glue layers together.

3. Referring to *Making Appliqués,* page 122, use patterns, page 116, to make one heart and two cheek appliqués for each gingerbread man ornament from fabric scraps. Position cheeks and heart on each gingerbread man; fuse in place. Glue three buttons onto each gingerbread man; use pen to draw "stitches," eyes, and mouths.

4. Arrange ornaments, pinecones, and sprigs of statice on wreath; glue in place.

5. Following *Making a Bow,* page 123, tie a 68" length of jute into a bow with six 8" loops and two 20" streamers. Position bow and streamers on wreath; glue in place.

WELCOMING COMMITTEE

*E*ven if you won't have a white Christmas, you can share some snowy fun with visitors when you add this friendly character to your welcoming committee. Our easy-to-finish snowman is crafted from an ordinary fence picket and "dressed" with a stocking cap and a fringed fabric scarf.

WHAT TO BUY
6-ft. fence picket, white spray paint, artificial textured snow, ¼ yd. of fabric, stocking cap, plastic foam carrot, and a small artificial poinsettia

THINGS YOU HAVE AT HOME
Handsaw, sandpaper, paintbrush, utility knife, fourteen assorted black buttons, two small branches, and a hot glue gun

SNOWMAN PICKET

Allow paint to dry after each application.

1. Use handsaw to cut 1 ft. from fence picket. Sand board smooth.

2. Spray picket with one or two coats of paint. Use paintbrush to apply artificial snow to one side (front) of picket; allow to dry.

3. Tear a 1"w strip from long edge of fabric; cut strip into eight 5" long pieces. Use one piece to tie a knot around center of remaining pieces; glue to top of cap. Glue poinsettia to cuff of cap. Place cap on one end of picket.

4. Use knife to cut off large end of carrot, leaving flat surface. Glue carrot and nine buttons onto picket for face.

5. Fray edges of remaining fabric piece; tie around picket for scarf.

6. Glue remaining buttons onto picket below scarf.

7. Glue branches to back of picket for arms.

WOODLAND ELEGANCE

*E*njoy the rustic beauty of the North Woods with this designer-look wreath! We embellished a plain grapevine circlet with holly, evergreens, and a variety of naturals, including nuts, berries, and sweet gum balls.

WHAT TO BUY
16" dia. grapevine wreath, preserved holly leaves, and ¹/₂ lb. of mixed nuts

THINGS YOU HAVE AT HOME
Spanish moss, sprigs of pine and cedar with berries, sweet gum balls, raffia, and a hot glue gun

NATURAL WREATH
1. Arrange Spanish moss, holly leaves, and pine and cedar sprigs on wreath; glue in place. Arrange nuts, berries, and sweet gum balls in greenery on wreath; glue in place.

2. Tie raffia into a bow; glue to wreath.

JUMBO STOCKING

UNDER $5!

Santa can't miss this giant stocking! Trimmed with a jester-style cuff and patches at the heel and toe, our decorative felt stocking announces guests with a merry jingle. Best of all, you can create it for less than $5!

WHAT TO BUY
$1/2$ yd. of green felt, $3/8$ yd. of tan felt, gold embroidery floss, and five 25mm jingle bells

THINGS YOU HAVE AT HOME
Tracing paper; embroidery needle; three small boxes; scraps of assorted fabrics, natural raffia, jute twine, and wired ribbon; newspaper; pine greenery; and a hot glue gun

JUMBO STOCKING

Refer to Embroidery Stitches, page 124, before beginning project. Use six strands of floss for all stitching.

1. Following *Making Patterns,* page 122, trace patterns, pages 117, 118, and 119 onto tracing paper. Using patterns, cut two stockings from green felt. Cut a 1" x 5" rectangle for hanger, two cuffs, two toes, and two heels from tan felt.

2. For each side of stocking, pin heel and toe in place on stocking; work Running Stitch along inside edges of each. Matching wrong sides, pin stocking front

and back together. Pin cuffs to outside top edges. Leaving top open, work Blanket Stitch around all outside edges of stocking.

3. Matching short edges, fold hanger in half and stitch ends to inside top of stocking at back seam. Use floss to sew jingle bells to five points of cuff on stocking front.

4. For presents, wrap each box in a scrap of fabric; glue in place. Tie raffia, jute, or wired ribbon around wrapped boxes.

5. Stuff stocking lightly with newspaper. Arrange presents and greenery in top of stocking.

SLEEPY SANTA

*O*ur sleepy crescent Santa lends unique charm to any door! He's made using simple felt shapes, and lamb's wool adds a soft touch to his cap. A sprig of faux holly leaves and berries finishes this "ho-ho-homemade" decoration.

WHAT TO BUY

$1/8$ yd. of artificial lamb's wool; $2/3$ yd. of red felt; $1/3$ yd. of ecru felt; tan felt piece; ecru, red, and black embroidery floss; and a small artificial holly pick

THINGS YOU HAVE AT HOME

Tracing paper, newspaper, 22" square of corrugated cardboard, craft knife, fabric marking pencil, pins, embroidery needle, craft glue, wire cutters, floral wire, and a hot glue gun

CRESCENT SANTA DOOR DECORATION

Before beginning project, refer to Embroidery Stitches, page 124. Use three strands of floss for all stitching. Use craft glue for all gluing unless otherwise indicated.

1. Trace patterns, page 111, onto tracing paper; cut out. Using patterns, cut pom-pom and hat trim from lamb's wool and face from tan felt.

2. Use black floss to work Backstitch and Straight Stitch for eye and eyelashes.

3. Refer to *Cutting a Fabric Circle*, page 123, to cut 18" and 12" dia. circle patterns from newspaper.

4. Draw around 18" circle pattern on cardboard. Position 12" circle pattern $1/4$" from edge of 18" circle (Fig. 1); draw around pattern.

Fig. 1

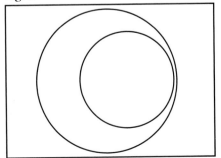

5. Position face, hat trim, and pom-pom patterns over drawn circles; draw around patterns on cardboard. Use craft knife to cut out cardboard shape as indicated by dashed lines in Fig. 2.

Fig. 2

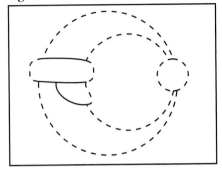

6. Position cardboard shape on red felt. Use fabric marking pen to draw around cardboard shape; cut out. Glue felt shape to front of cardboard shape.

7. For beard, draw around bottom half of crescent on ecru felt; cut out.

8. Arrange face, hat trim, pom-pom and beard on crescent; glue in place.

9. Use ecru floss to work Blanket Stitch around edges of beard and red floss to work Blanket Stitch around edges of hat.

10. Glue holly on hat trim.

11. For hanger, cut a 6" piece of floral wire; bend in half. Hot glue wire ends to back of crescent.

13

ALL THAT GLITTERS

*O*n this elegant tree, all that glitters is gold — ribbon, that is! You can craft this tastefully rustic decoration for a lot less than you'd think — gather twigs from your yard to assemble the "tree"; then add gleaming bows and painted bottle cap "ornaments."

WHAT TO BUY

Spray primer, gold and red spray paint, red and green dimensional paint, and 1½"w gold mesh wired ribbon (5-yd. spool)

THINGS YOU HAVE AT HOME

Soda bottle caps, hand saw, twigs, jute twine, floral wire, and wood glue

TWIG TREE

Allow paint to dry after each color application.

1. Spray each bottle cap with primer. Paint caps gold and red. Referring to *Painting Basics*, page 122, use dimensional paint to paint details on bottle caps.

2. For tree frame, cut a 28" length from a 1" dia. branch. Cut one 17" length and two 21" lengths from twigs. Arrange twigs; tie together with twine as shown in Fig. 1.

Fig. 1

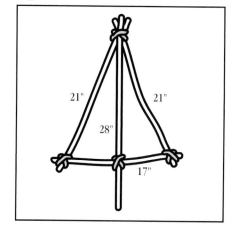

3. Beginning at top of tree, cut twigs into graduated lengths to fit across width of tree frame. Glue twigs in place on tree frame; allow to dry.

4. Cut ribbon into fourteen 12" lengths. Fold each length into a bow; twist floral wire around center of bow to secure.

5. Glue bows and bottle caps to tree.

6. Wrap bottom of trunk with ribbon; glue in place.

7. For hanger, form a 6" length of floral wire into a loop. Wrap wire ends around top of tree frame.

STARS OF GOLD

This gleaming wreath has the look of burnished gold — but it's amazingly affordable to make. The textured stars are cut from poster board, drizzled with hot glue, and painted to achieve a gilded effect. A gilt-edge bow adds the finishing touch.

WHAT TO BUY
14" dia. flat wire wreath form, white poster board, gold and black acrylic paint, 2 yds. of 1¹/₂"w ribbon, and a sprig of artificial holly

THINGS YOU HAVE AT HOME
Paintbrush, craft wire, tracing paper, craft knife, paper towel, and a hot glue gun

GOLD STAR WREATH

1. Paint wreath form gold.

2. Cut a 4" piece of craft wire; wrap ends around wreath form for hanger.

3. Trace star pattern, page 121, onto tracing paper; cut out. Draw around pattern 22 times on poster board.

4. Drizzle hot glue onto each star as desired; allow to dry. Use craft knife to cut out stars.

5. Paint front and back of each star gold, allow to dry. Thin black paint with a few drops of water. For antique look, lightly paint over each star with thinned paint. While paint is still wet, wipe off excess with paper towel.

6. Leaving ¹/₂" between stars, glue nine stars around wreath. Glue remaining stars on wreath, covering gaps in first layer.

7. Follow *Making a Bow,* page 123, and use ribbon to tie a bow with six loops and two 8" long streamers. Glue holly sprig to center of bow; glue bow to wreath.

15

*D*isplay "heart-felt" wishes with this folksy wreath. Perky gingerbread men and jolly Santas make fun decorations for the wreath, which is made by tying strips of felt to a wire foundation.

WHAT TO BUY

1 yd. of green felt; one white, one flesh, one black, two tan, and three red felt pieces; red and black embroidery floss; six black beads; 1/2 yd. of 5/8"w red ribbon; white baby rickrack; and a 12" dia. wire wreath form

THINGS YOU HAVE AT HOME

Tracing paper, pinking shears, embroidery needle, paper-backed fusible web, thread, assorted small white buttons, wire cutters, floral wire, and a hot glue gun

JOLLY FELT WREATH

Refer to Embroidery Stitches, page 124, before beginning project. Use six strands of floss for all stitching.

1. Fuse both tan felt pieces together; fuse two red felt pieces together.

2. Trace Santa, boots, and gingerbread boy patterns, page 105, onto tracing paper; cut out. Draw around gingerbread boy pattern three times on fused tan felt and Santa pattern three times on fused red felt. Using boots pattern, cut three shapes from black felt. Cut out Santas. Use pinking shears to cut out gingerbread boys.

3. Carefully separate layers of felt at bottom of Santa body. Position boots between layers; pin in place.

4. Use black floss to work Blanket Stitch around edge of Santas, French Knots for eyes, and Straight Stitch for noses. Use red floss to work Backstitch for gingerbread boy mouths. Sew beads to gingerbread boys for eyes.

5. Follow *Making Appliqués*, page 122, and use patterns, page 105, to make three each of beard, mustache, pom-pom appliqués, and six cuff appliqués using pinking shears to cut out cuffs and pom-poms. Arrange appliqués on each Santa; fuse in place.

6. Cut three 19" lengths of rickrack. Hand sew one length to edge of each gingerbread boy. For bow ties, cut three 6" lengths of ribbon. Fold each length into a bow, wrapping red floss around center to secure; glue one bow to each figure.

7. Sew buttons on front of each figure.

8. For wreath, use pinking shears to cut green felt into 1" x 6" strips. Make a 1" lengthwise cut in center of each strip. Fold each strip around wire, pulling one end of strip through cut in center of strip (Fig. 1). Repeat with each strip until wreath form is covered.

Fig. 1

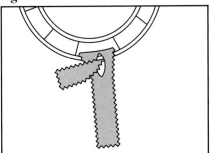

9. Cut six 5" lengths of floral wire. Glue center of wire to center back of each figure. Thread wire ends through wreath, twisting at back of wreath to secure.

10. For bow, use pinking shears and remaining red felt piece to cut two 1/2" x 10" strips for loops, two 1/2" x 41/2" strips for streamers, and one 1" x 31/2" strip for bow center. Cut a 1" x 8" strip. Wrap strip around top of wreath; overlap and glue ends in place. Assemble bow and glue together. Glue knot of bow to front of strip.

Deck
THE HALLS

Come along with us and see how inexpensively you can dress every room in the house in festive style. You'll love the appliquéd card "clothesline," and we've given lots of ideas for stockings to hang. You can whip up colorful pillows for any spot, step into the den to skirt the tree, or "get cooking" in the kitchen with decorative accents. And if you're ready for more, you can carry Christmas cheer into the garden with painted stepping stones. Who says you have to skimp on decorations to keep from breaking your budget!

EASY KITCHEN ACCENT

*S*tart your holiday decorating from the ground up with this easy no-sew floorcloth! Fusing simple fabric cutouts to a plain purchased mat creates a great Christmas decoration that's useful, too.

WHAT TO BUY
20" x 34" half-round canvas floorcloth and ⅛ yd. each of red and green fabrics

THINGS YOU HAVE AT HOME
Paper-backed fusible web

APPLIQUÉD FLOORCLOTH
1. Follow *Making Appliqués*, page 122, and use patterns, page 106, to make bow, bow center, holly, and berry appliqués from fabrics.

2. Cut 1¼" x 38" strips from fabric and fusible web; fuse together. Cut strip into 2" lengths.

3. Arrange appliqués and strips on floorcloth; fuse in place.

FROSTY TRIO

*A*ccented with folksy fabric patches and buttons, this holiday stocking will add frosty charm to the mantel. The cuff features a jolly trio of cross-stitched snowmen and is finished with colorful cord edgings.

WHAT TO BUY

8" x 10" piece of 14 count white Aida, embroidery floss (see chart and color key, page 104), Christmas stocking with cuff, $1/8$ yd. of Christmas fabric, and 1 yd. of $6/32$"w cord

THINGS YOU HAVE AT HOME

Thread, sharp needle, pinking shears, paper-backed fusible web, and assorted red and green buttons

CROSS-STITCHED SNOWMEN STOCKING

Refer to Cross Stitch, page 125, before beginning project.

1. Use a wide zigzag stitch to sew around raw edges of Aida.

2. Use three strands of floss to stitch design (chart and color key, page 104).

3. Trim Aida to $7/8$" above design and $3/4$" below design.

4. Measure around cuff of stocking. Cut two lengths of cord the determined measurement; cut two strips of fabric $1 1/2$" by the determined measurement. Position cord on wrong side of each fabric strip. Fold strip over cord. Use a zipper foot to baste close to cord along length of strip. Matching right sides and long edges, use a $3/8$" seam allowance to sew cord to top and bottom of Aida band. Turn edges to wrong side; press.

5. Centering band on cuff of stocking with stitched design at center front, stitch in place close to cord.

6. For patches, cut $2 1/2$" squares from fusible web, Aida, and fabric. Fuse web to wrong sides of Aida and fabric. Use pinking shears to trim $1/4$" from edges of fabric square and $3/8$" from edges of Aida. Fuse patches to stocking front.

7. Sew buttons to stocking.

"ILLUMINATED" PLACE MATS

Create cozy place settings at your Yuletide table with our soft, fleecy place mats. Each mat is "illuminated" with a string of light bulb appliqués and then edged with simple blanket stitching. A set of four also makes a great gift!

WHAT TO BUY
¹/₂ yd. of red thermal fleece; green yarn; yellow, green, blue, and black felt pieces; and yellow, green, blue, and black embroidery floss

THINGS YOU HAVE AT HOME
Yarn needle, tracing paper, embroidery needle, and thread

FLEECE PLACE MATS
Refer to Embroidery Stitches, page 124, before beginning project.

1. For four place mats, cut four 11¹/₂" x 18¹/₂" rectangles from fleece.

2. Use yarn needle and yarn to work Blanket Stitch around edge of each place mat.

3. Trace patterns, page 109, onto tracing paper; cut out. Using patterns, cut four bulbs each from yellow, green, and blue felt and twelve sockets from black felt.

4. For light string, arrange a 33" length of yarn on each place mat. Use thread to work Couching Stitch to secure yarn.

5. Arrange sockets and bulbs along light string. Use three strands of matching floss to work Blanket Stitch around edges of bulbs and sockets.

NO PEEKIN'!

Expect to Spend

felt	.40
embroidery floss	.20
cord	.24
jingle bells	.50
Total	**$1.34**

*K*eep curious eyes from peeking at Santa's work with this petite door pillow. Trimming the bottom edge of the hanger, jingle bells are ready to sound the alarm that little ones are spying, hoping for a midnight glimpse!

WHAT TO BUY
Green and dark green felt pieces, red embroidery floss, ¹/₂ yd. of decorative cord, and nine 12mm gold jingle bells

THINGS YOU HAVE AT HOME
Tracing paper, embroidery needle, thread, three red buttons, and polyester fiberfill

"NO PEEKIN'" DOOR HANGER
Refer to Embroidery Stitches, page 124, before beginning project. Use six strands of floss for all stitching unless otherwise indicated.

1. Cut two 6" squares from green felt. Trace patterns, page 114, onto tracing paper. Using leaf pattern, cut four shapes from dark green felt.

2. Pin "No Peekin'" pattern onto one felt square. Stitching through pattern, work Couching Stitch, French Knot, and Straight Stitch to embroider words onto felt. Carefully tear away tracing paper.

3. Matching right sides and leaving an opening for stuffing, sew felt squares

together. Clip corners and turn right side out. Sew leaves and buttons to top corner of pillow front. Stuff pillow with fiberfill; sew opening closed.

4. Tie a knot 1" from each end of cord; fray ends. Sew knots of cord to top corners of pillow.

5. Using three strands, thread needle with a 36" length of floss. For jingle bell fringe, secure floss at bottom corner of pillow. Bring needle through edge to front. Thread one bell onto floss. Bring needle through edge of pillow to form a ¹/₂" loop

(Fig. 1). Bring needle around loop, catching floss under needle and tie a knot at top of loop (Fig. 2).

Fig. 1

(Continued on page 95)

23

DINING ROOM DAZZLE

*Y*our table will truly sparkle when you dress it up with this extraordinary table runner. It's simple to cut motifs from Christmas fabric and fuse them to an inexpensive purchased runner. What an economical way to add dazzle to the dining room!

WHAT TO BUY

Table runner with tassels, ¼ yd. of poinsettia print Christmas fabric, and gold dimensional paint

THINGS YOU HAVE AT HOME

Paper-backed fusible web

POINSETTIA TABLE RUNNER

1. Fuse web to wrong side of fabric. Cut desired designs from fabric; fuse to each end of table runner.

2. Referring to *Painting Basics,* page 122, paint over edges of appliqués; allow to dry.

24

POSH POINSETTIA PILLOW

*T*his color-splashed accent commands attention! No one will guess that it cost less than $6 to dress up one of your everyday throw pillows. The cover is easy to craft using floral print napkins and golden ribbon — and there's no sewing involved!

WHAT TO BUY

Two Christmas print 16¹⁄₂" square cloth napkins, one red 16¹⁄₂" square cloth napkin, and 3 yds. of ¹⁄₄"w gold ribbon

THINGS YOU HAVE AT HOME

Square throw pillow (we used a 14" pillow) and seven safety pins

PILLOW COVER

1. Cut ribbon into six 18" lengths. For each bow set, tie one ribbon length into a bow. Tie another ribbon length into a bow around knot of previous bow.

2. Overlapping edges of print napkins 1³⁄₄", place wrong side up on a flat surface. Center pillow on napkins. Place red napkin over top of pillow. Bring ends

(Continued on page 91)

O HOLY NIGHT

*Y*ou'll want to find a special place for this exquisite luminary! Using glass etching paint, silhouettes of the Holy Family are cast onto a simple hurricane globe. It will be a resplendent centerpiece for your holiday decor.

WHAT TO BUY
8¹/₂"h glass hurricane globe, clear Con-tact™ paper, Delta™ Perm Enamel White Frost Glass Etching Paint, and a 4"h white candle

THINGS YOU HAVE AT HOME
Fine-point permanent pen; craft knife; clean, dry paintbrush; denatured alcohol; unused, smooth-textured sponge; and a tapestry needle

ETCHED NATIVITY GLOBE
1. Wash hurricane globe with soapy water; rinse and dry thoroughly. For ground portion of scene, cut a piece of Con-tact™ paper to fit around bottom half of globe. Cut a gentle wave pattern along top edge of paper piece; adhere to globe.

2. Use pen to trace pattern, page 101, onto plastic side of a second piece of Con-tact™ paper. Remove paper backing and position on globe, slightly overlapping top edge of first paper piece. Use craft knife to carefully cut around designs;

remove excess Con-tact™ paper (background).

3. To condition globe, use paintbrush to apply alcohol to surface; allow to air dry.

4. Using sponge, follow manufacturer's instructions to apply etching paint over design on globe. Allow to dry for two hours; remove patterns. To create stars, halo, and star rays, use needle to scratch designs in etching paint.

5. Place candle inside globe.

26

IT'S "CHRISTMAS-THYME"

UNDER $5!

*O*ur country Christmas angel will bring a touch of homespun charm to the kitchen. Because she's made with naturals and simple materials, you can craft her for a surprising $2.18!

WHAT TO BUY
¹/₃ yd. of muslin; yellow, red, green, and brown embroidery floss; and a small artificial bird

THINGS YOU HAVE AT HOME
Tracing paper, embroidery needle, thread, blush for cheeks, polyester fiberfill, a tapestry needle, three buttons, one 12" twig, two 8" twigs, two 8" cedar branches, jute twine, and a hot glue gun

CHRISTMAS KITCHEN ANGEL

Refer to Embroidery Stitches, page 124, before beginning project. Use six strands of floss for all stitching.

1. Trace patterns, page 99, onto tracing paper. Using head pattern, cut two shapes from muslin. Pin face pattern to one muslin shape. Stitching through pattern, work Running Stitch for eyebrows and nose and French Knots for eyes. Work Straight Stitch for mouth; carefully tear away pattern. Apply blush to cheeks.

2. Matching right sides and leaving neck open for stuffing, sew head shapes

(Continued on page 91)

*Y*ou'll have a down-home holiday when you make our pretty patchwork pieces part of your decor. Surround the tree with the cheery skirt, and be sure to hang the stocking where Santa can fill it with holly-jolly treats!

WHAT TO BUY
20" x 30" kitchen towels (package of five assorted)

THINGS YOU HAVE AT HOME
Seam ripper, thread, thumbtack, string, fabric marking pen, and assorted white buttons

PATCHWORK STOCKING AND TREE SKIRT

Use a ¹/₄" seam allowance for all sewing unless otherwise indicated.

1. For stocking hanger and cuff, cut a 4"w strip from finished end of one towel; set aside.

2. Use seam ripper to remove hems from towels; press towels flat. Cut 72 six-inch squares from towels.

3. For stocking, cut twelve assorted 6" squares into 3" squares. (Reserve remaining 6" squares for tree skirt.) To make pieced section for stocking front, refer to Fig. 1 to sew twenty 3" squares together. Reversing layout, repeat for stocking back.

Fig. 1

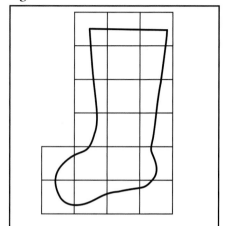

4. Trace stocking pattern, page 113, onto tracing paper. Place pieced sections right sides together and use pattern to cut out stocking front and back. Leaving top edge open, sew front and back together.

5. For hanger, cut a 2" x 12" piece from unhemmed edge of reserved towel strip. Press each long edge ¹/₄" to wrong side. Matching wrong sides and long edges, fold piece in half. Topstitch along pressed edge. Sew raw ends of hanger to inside back seam of stocking.

6. For stocking cuff, cut remainder of reserved strip to measure 2" x 14¹/₄". Turn short edges ¹/₄" to wrong side; press. Turn ¹/₄" again; sew in place.

7. Aligning short hemmed edges of cuff with back seam of stocking, match right side raw edge of cuff to wrong side top edge of stocking; pin in place. Sew cuff and stocking together. Fold cuff over to right side of stocking. Sew buttons to cuff.

8. For tree skirt, sew eight 6" squares (reserved in Step 3) together to make Row A. Make six Row A's. Sew six 6" squares together to make Row B. Make two Row B's. Referring to Fig. 2, sew Row A's and Row B's together to make pieced section.

Fig. 2

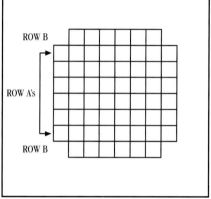

ROW B

ROW A's

ROW B

9. Follow *Cutting a Fabric Circle*, page 123, to cut a 44" dia. circle from pieced section; repeat to cut a 6" dia. inner circle. For opening at back of tree skirt, cut open one seam from inner circle to outer edge.

10. Press all raw edges ¹/₂" to wrong side. Topstitch in place.

HANGIN' AROUND

*L*et this frosty fellow hang around your kitchen! Our friendly snowman hanger is easy to sew from felt and attach to an ordinary dish towel. He'll be a jolly — and useful — accent!

WHAT TO BUY

15$\frac{1}{2}$" x 16" kitchen towel; one blue, one orange, two white, and two red felt pieces; orange, blue, and black embroidery floss; two $\frac{3}{4}$" dia. black shank buttons; and 1 yd. of $\frac{5}{8}$"w red grosgrain ribbon

THINGS YOU HAVE AT HOME

Thread, tracing paper, batting, six assorted black buttons, clear nylon thread, and an embroidery needle

SNOWMAN DISH TOWEL

Refer to Embroidery Stitches, page 124, before beginning project. Use three strands of floss for all stitching.

1. Baste along one short end of towel; pull thread to gather towel edge to measure 5$\frac{1}{2}$". Knot thread ends and adjust gathers evenly.

2. Trace patterns, page 120, onto tracing paper. Using patterns, cut one nose from orange felt, two heads from white felt, two hatbands from blue felt, and two hats from red felt. Cut one hat and one head from batting.

3. Sew shank buttons for eyes and assorted black buttons for mouth to one head shape. Pin nose in place; use orange floss to work Blanket Stitch around edges of nose.

4. Pin hatbands to hat shapes. Using blue floss, work Blanket Stitch along edges of hatbands.

5. Position batting shapes between head and hat shapes and gathered end of towel between layers at bottom of head.

6. Cut ribbon in half. Position one end of each ribbon piece between layers at top of hat; pin in place.

7. Use clear nylon thread to machine stitch through all layers around edges of head and hat.

8. Tie ribbons into a bow.

PLACE MAT PILLOW

*I*t's a snap to create a home accent that's super budget-friendly! Using ready-made place mats featuring holiday motifs, you can quickly stitch together this comfy throw pillow. It'll look great in any nook or cranny!

WHAT TO BUY
Two Christmas tapestry place mats and polyester fiberfill

THINGS YOU HAVE AT HOME
Thread

TAPESTRY PILLOW
1. Matching wrong sides and leaving an opening for stuffing, sew place mats together.

2. Stuff with fiberfill; sew opening closed.

SHADES OF CHRISTMAS

*D*ress up ordinary candlestick lamps for the holidays with these fabric-covered lampshades. You can choose from two festive finishes — miniature ornaments or an elegant gold bow. What a quick and inexpensive way to sprinkle a little Christmas cheer around your home!

WHAT TO BUY
Ornament Shade:
3" x 4¹/₂" x 5" lampshade, ¹/₄ yd. of fabric, twelve 15mm plastic Christmas ball ornaments, and ³/₄ yd. of ¹/₈"w gold cord

Bow Shade:
3" x 4¹/₂" x 5" lampshade, ¹/₄ yd. of fabric, ³/₄ yd. of 1¹/₂"w gold ribbon, and ³/₄ yd. of ¹/₄"w gold trim

THINGS YOU HAVE AT HOME
Tissue paper, tape, spray adhesive, gold thread, craft glue, and a hot glue gun

CHRISTMAS LAMPSHADES
1. Follow *Covering a Lampshade,* page 123, to cover each shade with fabric.

2. For ornament lampshade, thread one 3" length of gold thread through loop of each ornament. Spacing ornaments evenly, hot glue thread ends inside bottom of lampshade. Beginning and ending at seam of fabric, use craft glue to glue cord around top and bottom of shade.

3. For bow shade, glue trim around top and bottom of shade. Tie ribbon into a bow around shade; use hot glue to secure.

ELEGANT VOTIVES

*T*ransform ordinary votive candles into elegant accents in just a few easy steps! The gold-painted seals are made by "embossing" hot glue with a fancy spoon handle.

WHAT TO BUY
Two votive cups with candles, 1 yd. of ⁵/₈"w wired ribbon, and gold acrylic paint

THINGS YOU HAVE AT HOME
Waxed paper, an old spoon with decorative handle, and a hot glue gun

BERIBBONED CANDLES
1. Measure around votive. Cut a length of ribbon the determined measurement; glue ribbon around votive. Cut a 4¹/₂" length of ribbon. Form ribbon as desired; center and glue over ribbon ends on votive.

2. Squeeze a nickel-size amount of glue onto waxed paper. While glue is still warm, press end of spoon handle into glue. Allow glue to cool slightly; remove spoon. Paint seal; allow to dry. Glue seal to center of ribbon.

JOLLY SAINT NICK

*J*olly Saint Nick is here to greet guests from near and far! This simple wool Santa features felt and button accents that are attached with a childlike touch. His primitive look will add old-timey flair to any holiday home.

WHAT TO BUY

$1/2$ yd. of red wool fabric, $1/8$ yd. of ecru wool fabric, pink felt piece, and black embroidery floss

THINGS YOU HAVE AT HOME

Thread, resealable sandwich bag, gravel or sand, plastic grocery bags, rubber band, jute twine, drawing compass, tracing paper, embroidery needle, polyester fiberfill, pinking shears, assorted buttons, and a hot glue gun

PRIMITIVE SANTA

1. For Santa body, cut a 16" x 22" rectangle from red wool. Matching right sides and short edges, fold rectangle in half. Using a $1/2$" seam allowance, sew along one side and one end of body; turn right side out.

2. Fill sandwich bag half full with gravel; seal bag. Place bag in bottom of Santa body. Stuff body with grocery bags to within 3" from top. Gather opening and wrap with rubber band to close. Tie a 15" length of twine around gathers, covering rubber band.

3. Use compass and tracing paper to make a $4^{1}/_{2}$" dia. pattern for snowman head and hat. Trace nose and cheek patterns, page 110, onto tracing paper. Using patterns, cut two heads from ecru wool, one hat from red wool, and one nose and two cheeks from pink felt.

4. Use embroidery floss to work long straight stitches for mouth and to sew cheeks and nose onto one head shape. Working from right side, take a small stitch for each eye. Leaving a 3" tail at each end of stitch, tie floss into a double knot. Trim floss ends $1/8$" from knot.

5. Matching wrong sides and leaving an opening for stuffing, use floss to whipstitch head pieces together. Stuff with fiberfill; sew opening closed. Glue head onto gathers of body.

6. Use pinking shears to cut two 2" x 6" strips from red wool and seven 1" x 6" strips from ecru wool. For each arm, tie a knot 1" from one end of one red strip; glue opposite end to side of body. For beard, fold six ecru wool strips in half and glue along bottom of face. For

(Continued on page 95)

34

WINTRY WHIMSY

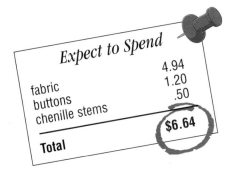
A whimsical orange nose and a bow-tied top hat make this fun fellow a great way to dress up the mantel! Inexpensive corduroy and flannel give the stocking a cuddly look — as well as an attractive price.

WHAT TO BUY

$3/8$ yd. of ecru corduroy, $1/4$ yd. of black corduroy, $1/8$ yd. of flannel, two $5/8$" dia. black buttons, five $1/2$" dia. black buttons, and orange bump chenille stems

THINGS YOU HAVE AT HOME

Tracing paper; white, orange, and black thread; and a pencil

CORDUROY SNOWMAN STOCKING

Use a $1/4$" seam allowance for all sewing unless otherwise indicated.

1. Trace patterns, page 102, onto tracing paper. Using patterns, cut two stocking shapes (one in reverse) from ecru corduroy and two hat shapes from black corduroy.

2. Matching right sides, sew stocking front and back together. Clip seams along curves; turn right side out.

3. Matching right sides, sew side edges of hat together; clip corners. Turn bottom edge of hat $1/4$" to wrong side; stitch in place. Turn hat right side out.

4. To attach hat to stocking, place hat inside stocking, matching right side of hat to wrong side of stocking and matching top edges and side seams. Stitch together along top edges; turn hat out over stocking.

5. Sew $5/8$" dia. buttons to stocking for eyes and $1/2$" dia. buttons to stocking for mouth. For nose, curl chenille stem around a pencil; use orange thread to sew in place on snowman face.

(Continued on page 92)

HAPPY HOLIDAY FRIEND

*F*olks are sure to warm up to this happy homespun snowman. Made of corduroy and tied with a flannel scarf, our country accent will complement your decor — and your budget!

WHAT TO BUY
1/2 yd. of ecru corduroy, polyester fiberfill, orange felt piece, and black embroidery floss

THINGS YOU HAVE AT HOME
Thread, resealable sandwich bag, gravel or sand, 10" long twig, rubber band, drawing compass, tracing paper, two 5/8" dia. black buttons, thread, embroidery needle, scrap of fabric for scarf, three assorted buttons, and a hot glue gun

COUNTRY CORDUROY SNOWMAN
1. For snowman body, cut a 16" x 22" rectangle from corduroy. Matching right sides and short edges, fold rectangle in half. Using a 1/2" seam allowance, sew along side and one end of body; turn right side out. For arms, cut a small hole in each side of body.

2. Fill sandwich bag half full with gravel; seal bag. Place bag in bottom of snowman body. Insert twig through holes for arms. Stuff body with fiberfill to within 3" from top. Wrap rubber band around top 3" of body; adjust gathers evenly.

3. Use compass and tracing paper to make a 4 1/2" dia. circle pattern for snowman head. Trace snowman nose pattern, page 100, onto tracing paper. Using patterns, cut two heads from corduroy and one nose from felt.

4. Matching long edges, fold nose in half. Use floss to sew long edges together; stuff nose with fiberfill. For face, sew nose and 5/8" black buttons for eyes to one head piece. Use floss and work Straight Stitch, page 125, to stitch mouth.

5. Matching wrong sides and leaving an opening for stuffing, use floss to whipstitch head pieces together. Stuff with fiberfill; sew opening closed. For "hair," pull a few strands of fiberfill to outside between stitching. Glue head to gathers at top of body.

6. Pull a small amount of fiberfill to outside of body at each arm opening.

7. For scarf, tear a 2 1/2" x 15" strip of fabric; knot around neck over rubber band.

8. Knotting ends at front of buttons and leaving long tails, use floss to sew remaining buttons to front of snowman.

HOLLY-BRIGHT TREE SKIRT

*F*or less than $10, you can add spirit to your holiday decor with our bright holly-trimmed tree skirt! Vibrant red corduroy and green felt come together to create an eye-catching Christmas decoration that you'll enjoy year after year.

WHAT TO BUY
Three green and three dark green felt pieces, 1¹⁄₈ yds. of red corduroy, and three skeins of green embroidery floss

THINGS YOU HAVE AT HOME
Tracing paper, pinking shears, pencil, string, thumbtack, ¹⁄₂"w paper-backed fusible web tape, scraps of four different green fabrics, thread, and fabric glue

HOLLY TREE SKIRT
1. Trace patterns, page 101, onto tracing paper. Using leaf patterns, cut nine A's from dark green felt. Use pinking shears to cut nine B's from green felt. Center one A on each B and glue in place. Cut 23 C's from dark green felt. Use pinking shears to cut 23 D's from green felt. Center one C on each D and glue in place.

(Continued on page 92)

YULETIDE GREETINGS

*W*hat a creative way to display all the greeting cards we receive during the Yuletide! Use mini clothespins to clip cards to a ribbon "clothesline" held up by two happy gingerbread men.

WHAT TO BUY
$1/2$ yd. of fabric for background and hanging sleeve, $1/4$ yd. of fabric for border, $1/4$ yd. of fabric for binding, two wooden heart buttons, $1^1/2$"h alphabet stencil, 1 yd. of $1/8$"w red ribbon, mini clothespins, and a $3/8$" dia. wooden dowel

THINGS YOU HAVE AT HOME
Heavyweight fusible interfacing; paper-backed fusible web; scraps of Christmas print fabrics, tan fabric, red fabric, and white felt; $3/4$"w paper-backed fusible web tape; pinking shears; red and black embroidery floss; $1/4$" dia. hole punch; craft glue; paintbrush; red acrylic paint; two $3/4$" dia. buttons; and a pencil

CHRISTMAS CARD WALL HANGING
Refer to Embroidery Stitches, page 124, before beginning project. Use six strands of floss for all stitching.

1. For background, cut $12^1/2$" x 34" rectangles from fabric and interfacing. Fuse interfacing to wrong side of fabric.

2. For border, cut two $2^1/4$" x 34" and two $2^1/4$" x $12^1/2$" strips from fabric and fusible web. Fuse long strips to top and bottom and short strips to sides of background.

3. Follow *Making Appliqués*, page 122, to make four $2^1/4$" square appliqués from Christmas fabric; fuse one square to each corner of border.

4. For binding, cut two 2" x $13^1/2$" and two 2" x 34" strips from fabric. Press long edges of 34" strips $1/4$" to wrong side. Press short edges of $13^1/2$" strips $1/2$" to wrong side and long edges $1/4$" to wrong

(Continued on page 95)

SANTA'S PATHWAY

*H*ere's a fun idea for adding holiday spirit to your lawn. We used acrylic paint to decorate an inexpensive stepping stone. Why not make enough to create a path for Santa to follow to your door!

WHAT TO BUY
One 12" dia. concrete garden stone and white, flesh, red, and black acrylic paint

THINGS YOU HAVE AT HOME
Tracing paper, paintbrushes, black medium-point felt-tip marker, and clear acrylic spray sealer

GARDEN STONE SANTA
Allow paint to dry after each color application.

1. Referring to *Making Patterns,* page 122, trace patterns, page 98, onto tracing paper; cut out. Draw around patterns on garden stone, overlapping as necessary.

2. Paint designs. Mix small amounts of red and white paint together to paint Santa's nose, cheeks, and mouth. Use white paint to add highlights.

3. Use marker to add details to Santa and candy cane stripes on "HO HO HO."

4. Spray design with two or three coats of acrylic sealer.

REDWORK CHARM

*B*ring back the old-fashioned style of redwork embroidery with these amazingly economical stockings (you can make two for just over $4!). A Battenberg lace cuff stitched with a merry message adds antique charm to these mantel decorations.

WHAT TO BUY
$1/2$ yd. of fabric, 8" x 12" oval Battenberg doily, and red embroidery floss

THINGS YOU HAVE AT HOME
Tracing paper, transfer paper, thread, and embroidery needle

REDWORK STOCKINGS
Refer to Embroidery Stitches, page 124, before beginning project. Use two strands of floss for all stitching.

1. Referring to *Making Patterns*, page 122, trace stocking pattern, page 112, onto tracing paper. Using pattern, cut stocking front and back from fabric.

2. Matching right sides and leaving top edge open, use a $1/4$" seam allowance to sew stocking front and back together. Clip curves; turn stocking right side out and press. Turn top edge of stocking $1/2$" to inside; press. Turn pressed edge $1/2$" again and press. Sew around top of stocking $1/4$" below top edge.

3. For hanger, cut a 3" x 12" strip of fabric. Turn long edges of strip $3/4$" to wrong side; press. Matching turned edges, fold strip in half lengthwise; press. Sew along double folded edges. Fold strip in half to form a loop. Sew ends inside top of stocking at back seam.

4. Matching short ends, fold doily in half; cut doily along fold. Trace embroidery pattern, page 113, onto tracing paper. Transfer pattern onto right side of one doily half.

5. Embroider design using Stem Stitch, Backstitch, Lazy Daisy Stitch, and French Knot.

6. Match right side raw edge of doily to wrong side top edge of stocking front; sew in place. Turn doily out over front of stocking; press.

41

JINGLE BELL STOCKING

*C*rocheters will love this
oh-so-simple project. Our cheery
candy-striped stocking works up
in no time using only three colors
of yarn, and it costs only $4.50!
Little bows and bells provide
a merry jingle.

WHAT TO BUY
White, red, and green worsted weight yarn
(2 ounces of each) six ⅝" dia. gold jingle
bells, and 1½ yds. of ¼"w red grosgrain
ribbon

THINGS YOU HAVE AT HOME
Size H crochet hook and a yarn needle

CROCHETED STOCKING
*Refer to Crochet, page 126, before
beginning project.*

GAUGE
14 dc and 7 rows = 4"

With red, ch 12 loosely, place marker in
last ch made for Cuff placement, ch 36
loosely; being careful not to twist ch, join
with slip st to form a ring.

Rnd 1 (Right side): Ch 3 (counts as first
dc, now and throughout), dc in next ch
and in each ch around; join with slip st to
first dc: 48 dc.

Note: Loop a short piece of yarn around
any stitch to mark Rnd 1 as right side.

Rnd 2: Ch 3, dc in next dc and in each
dc around changing to white in last dc;
join with slip st to first dc.

Rnd 3: Ch 3, dc in next dc and in each
dc around; join with slip st to first dc.

Rnd 4: Ch 3, dc in next dc and in each
dc around changing to red in last dc; join
with slip st to first dc.

Rnd 5: Ch 3, dc in next dc and in each
dc around; join with slip st to first dc.

Rnds 6-19: Repeat Rnds 2-5, 3 times;
then repeat Rnds 2 and 3 once more.

Rnd 20 (Heel opening): Ch 24 loosely,
skip next 23 dc, slip st in next dc, ch 3,
dc in next 23 dc and in each ch around
changing to red in last dc; join with slip st
to first dc: 48 dc.

Rnd 21: Ch 3, dc in next dc and in each
dc around; join with slip st to first dc.

Rnds 22-27: Repeat Rnds 2-5 once, then
repeat Rnds 2 and 3 once more.

Rnd 28: Ch 3, dc in next dc and in each
dc around changing to green in last dc;
join with slip st to first dc.

Note: To work dc decrease (uses 2dc), ★
YO, insert hook in next dc, YO and pull
up a loop, YO and draw through two
loops on hook; repeat from ★ once
more, YO and draw through all three
loops on hook (counts as one dc).

Rnd 29: Ch 3, dc in next dc, dc decrease,
(dc in next 2 dc, dc decrease) around;
join with slip st to first dc: 36 dc.

Rnd 30: Ch 3, dc decrease, (dc in next
dc, dc decrease) around; join with slip st
to first dc: 24 dc.

Rnd 31: Ch 2, dc in next dc, dc decrease
around; join with slip st to first dc, finish
off leaving a long end for sewing.

Thread yarn needle with end and weave
through stitches on Rnd 31; gather tightly
and secure end.

HEEL
Rnd 1: With right side facing and
working in skipped dc on Rnd 19, join
green with slip st in same st as joining at
base of ch-24; ch 2, dc in next dc, (dc
decrease, dc in next 7 dc) twice, dc
decrease twice; working in free loops of
ch-24, dc decrease twice, dc in next 7
chs, dc decrease, dc in next 7 chs, dc
decrease twice; join with slip st to first dc:
38 dc.

Rnd 2: Ch 2, dc in next dc, dc decrease,
dc in next 11 dc, dc decrease 4 times, dc
in next 11 dc, dc decrease twice; join with
slip st to first dc: 30 dc.

Note: To work double decrease (uses next
three dc), ★ YO, insert hook in next dc,
YO and pull up a loop, YO and draw
through two loops on hook; repeat from

(Continued on page 94)

43

Gifts
FOR ALL

Tired of giving the same old stodgy neckties and fuzzy house shoes? We've got the solution all wrapped up! This year, you can create gifts that will get "two thumbs up" from everyone on your list — and save you money, too. You'll even discover how to package your gifts for special deliveries. Grab your glue gun and get started early; at these prices, you'll want to make great gifts for everyone you know!

FIRESIDE WRAP

Who doesn't enjoy curling up by the fire on a cold winter night! This handsome blanket is perfect for snuggling, and it's super simple to make with no machine sewing.

WHAT TO BUY

1¹/₂ yds. of 54"w wool plaid fabric, ecru and red felt pieces, and red embroidery floss

THINGS YOU HAVE AT HOME

Thread, tracing paper, and an embroidery needle

FESTIVE WOOL BLANKET

Refer to Embroidery Stitches, page 124, before beginning project. Use four strands of floss for all stitching.

1. Cut selvages from fabric. Sew 1¹/₂" from edges of fabric. Pull threads to fringe all edges of fabric to stitching line.

2. Trace patterns, page 99, onto tracing paper. Using patterns, cut two mittens and two flower centers from ecru felt and two cuffs and two flowers from red felt. Arrange shapes on one corner of blanket; pin in place.

3. Work Blanket Stitch around edges of cuffs, mittens, and flowers. Work Straight Stitch and Cross Stitch in flower centers.

ELEGANT WELCOME

*S*urprise a friend with this *fragrant wreath to greet the season. Our economical project combines the elegant look of shimmering gold ribbon with the delicate scent of potpourri for a unique Yuletide accent.*

WHAT TO BUY

$3/4$" x $8^7/8$" dia. foam wreath, $1/4$ yd. of fabric, potpourri, $5/8$ yd. of $1^1/2$"w gold ribbon, and 3 yds. of $1/4$"w gold trim

THINGS YOU HAVE AT HOME

6" length of floral wire and a hot glue gun

POTPOURRI WREATH

1. Tear fabric into seven $1^1/4$" x 44" strips. Wrap strips around wreath, gluing ends to secure.

2. Glue potpourri onto wreath, covering front and sides.

3. Tie gold ribbon into a bow. Cut a 27" length of trim; tie into a bow. Glue trim bow to knot of ribbon bow.

4. Wrap remaining trim around wreath; glue in place. Glue bows to top of wreath.

5. For hanger, bend floral wire in half; glue ends to top back of wreath.

TWO THUMBS UP

*Y*ou'll get "two thumbs up" when you give a pair of these warm-and-snuggly fleece mittens adorned with felt appliqués and buttons. Choose bright colors to reflect the fun of the season!

WHAT TO BUY
Green Mittens:

Green fleece mittens; white felt piece; white, orange, green, and black embroidery floss; and twelve ³/₈" dia. white buttons

Red Mittens:

Red fleece mittens, green and black felt pieces, ecru and green embroidery floss, and a package of assorted craft buttons

THINGS YOU HAVE AT HOME

Cardboard, tracing paper, and an embroidery needle

FESTIVE HOLIDAY MITTENS

Refer to Embroidery Stitches, page 124, before beginning project. Use three strands of floss for all stitching. To prevent catching back of mitten while stitching, place a piece of cardboard inside mitten.

(Continued on page 91)

48

HERE COMES SANTA CLAUS!

There'll be no doubt Santa's on his way when folks see baby in this adorable holiday romper! Using only a few paints, it's simple to embellish a store-bought outfit for a little one.

WHAT TO BUY
infant-size red romper and flesh and green acrylic paint

THINGS YOU HAVE AT HOME
Waxed paper, tracing paper, transfer paper, paintbrushes, white and black acrylic paint, and a black permanent fabric marker

SANTA ROMPER
1. Place a sheet of waxed paper inside romper.

2. Referring to making patterns, page 122, trace pattern, page 100, onto tracing paper. Transfer pattern to front of romper.

3. Paint Santa design. Use marker to outline painted design and hat. Use white paint to create swirls for beard, paint dots on hat, and highlight eyes.

Expect to Spend

frame	6.49
paint	1.94
stamps	1.28
Total	**$9.71**

*T*his holiday frame is sure to receive a "stamp" of approval! Use sandpaper to give a timeworn look to a wooden frame, then glue postage stamps and card stock strips to the borders. Special tidings written with a gold paint pen finish the project.

WHAT TO BUY

Wooden frame, gold and brown acrylic paint, and four Christmas stamps

THINGS YOU HAVE AT HOME

Paintbrush, sandpaper, card stock to match stamps, decorative-edge craft scissors, craft glue, gold paint pen, and acrylic spray sealer

POSTAGE STAMP FRAME

1. Referring to *Painting Basics*, page 122, paint frame brown; allow to dry. Lightly sand with sandpaper. Dry-brush frame with gold paint.

2. Adhere stamps to card stock and use craft scissors to cut out $1/4$" outside edges of stamp.

3. Cut one strip of card stock slightly shorter and narrower than each side of frame. Glue strips and stamps to frame.

4. Write desired message with pen. Spray frame with sealer.

YULETIDE MEMORIES

*G*ive a friend's Yuletide photos the attention they deserve on these festive memory pages! They're perfect backdrops for unforgettable moments.

WHAT TO BUY

Three sheets of acid-free decorative paper and three sheets of white, red, or green card stock

THINGS YOU HAVE AT HOME

Scissors, decorative-edge craft scissors, scrapbook album pages, glue stick, photographs, items to decorate pages (we used Christmas card cutouts and motifs, stickers, and scraps of paper), and a black permanent fine-point marker

MEMORY PAGES

1. For each page, use decorative-edge craft scissors to trim acid-free paper to fit album page. Glue paper to page.

2. Select desired photographs for each page. Use scissors or craft scissors to cut desired images from photographs.

3. Mat images by gluing to card stock and trimming $^{1}/_{8}$" to $^{1}/_{2}$" outside edge of images or by "framing" with cutouts from Christmas cards.

4. Arrange and glue matted photographs to pages. Add desired decorations to pages.

5. Use marker to write desired captions on each page.

SNOW FRIENDS

Hugged by a friendly snow couple, this basket will hold candy, Christmas cards, or odds and ends in wintertime style! The pleasant pals are made from socks and "dressed" in scraps of fabric.

WHAT TO BUY

One pair each of women's white and red socks with ribbing, 5mm black flat-back beads, $1/8$" dia. red pom-poms, and an oval basket (we used a 7" x $10^{1}/4$" basket)

THINGS YOU HAVE AT HOME

Polyester fiberfill; thread; red and black embroidery floss; embroidery needle; tracing paper; jute twine; drawing compass; scraps of lace trim, black felt, and fabric; and a hot glue gun

SNOW FRIENDS BASKET

Refer to Embroidery Stitches, page 124, before beginning project.

1. For each head, cut 3" from toe end of one white sock; set aside remainder. Stuff sock toe pieces with fiberfill. Hand sew openings closed.

2. For each face, glue two beads to head for eyes. Glue a pom-pom to each face for nose. Use three strands of black floss to work Stem Stitch for mouths.

3. For arms, cut ribbing from remainder of each sock; cut ribbing in half lengthwise. Matching right sides and long edges, sew $1/8$" from long edge and along one end of each arm, forming a tube; turn right side out. Stuff each arm with fiberfill. Hand sew opening closed.

4. Trace pattern, page 106, onto tracing paper. Using pattern, cut eight mittens from felt. Leaving straight edge open, use

(Continued on page 94)

REINDEER TREATS

Expect to Spend

bowl	.96
chenille stems	.50
ribbon	.36
wiggle eyes	.39
craft foam	.79
candy	1.98
Total	**$4.98**

UNDER $5!

Santa's favorite reindeer can't wait to deliver sweet treats to your friends! With the price less than $5 (and that's including the candy!), you'll want to make a whole herd of whimsical reindeer.

WHAT TO BUY
4" dia. glass ivy bowl, brown chenille stems, $^2/_3$ yd. of $^1/_4$"w red ribbon, 15mm wiggle eyes, red craft foam, and two 5.5-oz. bags of candy

THINGS YOU HAVE AT HOME
Scraps of natural raffia, black permanent felt-tip marker, and a hot glue gun

REINDEER CANDY BOWL
1. Cut two 8" and two 5" lengths of chenille stems. Twist one 5" length around each 8" length. Bend stems to make antlers. Glue one antler to each side of bowl.

2. Cut several 1$^1/_4$" lengths of raffia; center between antlers and glue just below rim of bowl.

3. Tie ribbon into a bow around rim of bowl, covering top ends of raffia.

4. For nose, cut a 1" dia. circle from craft foam. Glue nose and eyes to front of bowl, just below raffia.

5. Use marker to draw eyebrows and mouth on bowl.

6. Place candy in bowl.

FUNNY-FACE SNOWMAN

UNDER $5!

Looking for a an original (but economical) way to package your home-baked goodies? Then you'll love our funny-face snowman gift bags! For just $1.22 apiece, you can transform lunch sacks into creative characters.

WHAT TO BUY

White paper lunch bags (package of 50), white and black craft foam sheets, white paper doilies (package of 20), and two yds. of $1^{1}/_{2}$"w wired ribbon

THINGS YOU HAVE AT HOME

Drawing compass, $^{1}/_{4}$" dia. hole punch, scrap of pink construction paper, black felt-tip pen, jumbo craft stick, assorted small black buttons, and a hot glue gun

SNOWMAN GIFT BAGS

1. For each snowman head, use compass to draw a $2^{1}/_{4}$" dia. circle on white craft foam; cut out. Punch two holes from pink paper for cheeks; glue in place on face. Use pen to draw eyes and mouth.

2. For hat, cut a $^{1}/_{2}$" x $2^{1}/_{2}$" rectangle and a $1^{1}/_{2}$" square from black craft foam. Arrange hat pieces on snowman head; glue in place.

3. For arms, draw around craft stick on white craft foam; cut out.

4. For snowflakes, cut small shapes from doilies. Glue snowflakes to bag and hat. Glue buttons to bag.

5. Place gift in bag.

6. Fold each side of bag top toward center to form a point. Position arms at point and roll top of bag and arms down twice; glue in place. Glue head and hat to center top of bag.

7. For scarf, tie ribbon around snowman neck.

54

FUN ON THE GO

These festive characters are ready for fun on the go! Our felt Santas and gingerbread boy are simply fused to a plain canvas tote and edged with quaint blanket stitching for a fast finish.

WHAT TO BUY

13" x 17" white canvas tote bag; one white, one flesh, one tan, and two red felt pieces; red and black embroidery floss; four black beads; white baby rickrack; $1/2$"w green satin ribbon (10-yd. spool); and $1/8$"w green satin ribbon (10-yd. spool)

THINGS YOU HAVE AT HOME

Tracing paper, paper-backed fusible web, scrap of black felt, pinking shears, embroidery needle, thread, scrap of red ribbon, assorted white buttons, 1"w paper-backed fusible web tape, scrap of Christmas print fabric, and a hot glue gun

FUN FELT CANVAS TOTE BAG

Before beginning project, refer to Embroidery Stitches, page 124. Use six strands of floss for all stitching.

1. Matching short edges, fold tan felt piece in half; cut along fold. Fuse tan felt pieces together; fuse red felt pieces together.

2. Trace Santa, boots, and gingerbread boy patterns, page 105, onto tracing paper; cut out. Draw around gingerbread boy pattern on tan felt; draw around Santa pattern two times on red felt. Using boots pattern, cut two shapes from black felt. Cut out Santas. Use pinking shears to cut out gingerbread boy.

3. Carefully separate layers of felt at bottom of each Santa body. Position boots between layers; pin in place.

4. Use black floss to work Blanket Stitch around edges of Santas, French Knots for eyes, and Straight Stitch for noses. Use red floss to work Backstitch for gingerbread boy mouth. Sew beads to gingerbread boy for eyes.

5. Follow *Making Appliqués*, page 122, and use patterns, page 105, to make two each of beard, mustache, and pom-pom

(Continued on page 93)

*S*how off snapshots of holiday "stars" with this stand-up photo frame. The Ohio Star quilt-block border has a homey look that's perfect for any room!

WHAT TO BUY

$1/4$ yd. each of white and red fabric, black embroidery floss, 10" x $11^1/2$" piece of foam core board, white poster board, $1/3$ yd. of craft fleece, $1/8$ yd. of 1"w white grosgrain ribbon, and four 1" dia. buttons

THINGS YOU HAVE AT HOME

Thread, embroidery needle, craft knife, cutting mat, spray adhesive, tape, photograph, and a hot glue gun

QUILTED FRAME

Use $1/4$"w seam allowances for all sewing unless otherwise indicated.

1. For quilt block, cut white fabric as follows: Four 3" squares (A), one $6^1/4$" square cut twice diagonally (B), two $1^1/2$" x $10^1/2$" side sashing strips and two $1^1/2$" x $12^1/2$" top/bottom sashing strips. Cut red fabric as follows: Four $3^3/8$" squares, each cut diagonally once (C), and one 6" square (D).

2. Arrange quilt pieces as indicated in Fig. 1; sew together.

Fig. 1

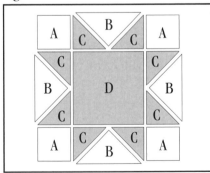

3. Sew side sashing strips, then top and bottom sashing strips to quilt block.

4. Using three strands of floss, work Running Stitch, page 124, around outside edges of red triangles. Cut an X in center square, cutting to within $1/16$" of each corner.

5. For frame, cut $9^3/4$" squares from foam core board, poster board, and fleece. Draw a line $2^3/8$" from each edge of foam core board and fleece squares, forming a 5" square in center of each; use craft knife to cut out squares. Use spray adhesive to attach fleece to foam core board.

6. Center quilt block right side up over fleece side of frame. Wrap all cut edges to back of frame, overlapping and trimming as necessary; glue in place.

7. Center photo behind opening of frame and tape in place. Glue poster board square to back of frame.

8. For frame stand, cut a $1^1/2$" x $9^1/4$" rectangle from foam core board. Make a cut in, but not through, frame stand $1/2$" from one end. Fold cut end to one side; glue to top center back of frame. Glue $1/2$" of one end of ribbon to underside of stand. Glue $1/2$" of opposite end to frame (Fig. 2).

Fig. 2

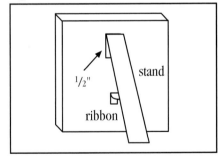

9. Center and glue one button on each front corner of frame.

ARTFUL ALBUM

*A*n ordinary greeting card provides the centerpiece for this artful photo album. Festive print fabric is used to cover the padded frame and make the easy-to-fuse appliqués. At about $6, this gift is a real pocketbook pleaser!

WHAT TO BUY

10¹/₄" x 11¹/₂" photo album, ¹/₃ yd. of green fabric, and a red felt piece

THINGS YOU HAVE AT HOME

Tracing paper, corrugated cardboard, scraps of red and green fabrics and batting, pinking shears, paper-backed fusible web, spray adhesive, 4" x 6" or larger greeting card, and a hot glue gun

HOLIDAY PHOTO ALBUM

1. Referring to *Making Patterns,* page 122, trace frame pattern, page 110, onto tracing paper; cut out. Draw around pattern on cardboard, batting, felt, and wrong side of purchased green fabric. Cut out cardboard and batting shapes along drawn lines. Use spray adhesive to attach batting to cardboard. Cut out fabric frame 1" outside drawn lines. Use pinking shears to cut out felt frame ¹/₄" outside drawn lines.

2. Follow *Making Appliqués,* page 122, and use patterns, page 110, to make eight (four in reverse) leaf and seventeen berry appliqués from fabric scraps.

Arrange appliqués at least 1¹/₄" from edges of green fabric frame; fuse in place.

3. Clip inner and outer corners of appliquéd fabric to within ¹/₄" of drawn lines (Fig. 1).

Fig. 1

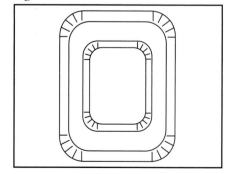

4. Apply spray adhesive to wrong side of appliquéd fabric. Center batting side of cardboard frame on wrong side of fabric. Smooth edges of fabric to back of cardboard frame; glue in place.

5. Center card in opening of felt frame; hot glue edges in place. Center felt frame with photo on album front; hot glue in place. Repeat to glue appliquéd frame over felt frame.

6. Fuse two 1¹/₂" x 16¹/₂" scraps of red fabric together. Use pinking shears to cut a 1" x 16" strip from fused fabric. Tie strip into a bow; glue to album.

58

*E*xpress your "thanks" and recycle favorite Christmas cards at the same time! Patterned tissue paper provides a backdrop for the festive motifs, which are glued to inexpensive note cards. Scraps of ribbon and greenery add the finishing touches.

WHAT TO BUY
4" x 5" note cards with envelopes

THINGS YOU HAVE AT HOME
Assorted tissue paper, craft glue, glue stick, Christmas cards, red and black permanent fine-point markers, and scraps of ribbon, and artificial greenery

THANK-YOU CARDS
Use glue stick for all gluing unless otherwise indicated.

1. For each card, tear a piece of tissue paper large enough to cover desired area on front of card. Glue tissue paper to card. If desired, glue a second piece of torn tissue paper or torn tissue paper strips to front or inside of card.

2. Cut desired motifs from Christmas cards. Glue motifs over tissue paper on front of card.

3. Use markers to write message on front or inside of card.

4. Tie a length of ribbon into a bow. Use craft glue to attach bow and greenery to card.

FUN PHOTO KEEPERS

Youngsters will have a ball decorating these photo books to give to their friends! Grown-ups can help cover plain albums with scraps cut from paper grocery bags, then let the kids add handwritten messages and trims cut from scrapbook paper. What fun (and inexpensive) gifts!

WHAT TO BUY

Two 5" x 7" photo books and seven assorted sheets of scrapbook paper

THINGS YOU HAVE AT HOME

Brown paper grocery bags, spray adhesive, tracing paper, 1/4" dia. hole punch, black felt-tip pen, and craft glue

KIDS' PHOTO BOOKS

1. For photo book cover, draw around open book on grocery bag; cut 1/2" outside drawn line.

2. Clipping corners and folding edges to inside of photo book, use spray adhesive to glue cover in place. Cut two 5" x 6" pieces from paper bag; glue to inside front and back covers of photo book.

3. Piecing as necessary, cut 3/8"w strips of decorative scrapbook paper; glue in place along borders of photo book.

4. Trace patterns, page 116, onto tracing paper. Using patterns, cut tree and snowman from scrapbook paper. For tree "ornaments," punch holes from desired colors of paper. Glue shapes onto front of book.

5. Use pen to write desired message and draw details.

HANDMADE GREETINGS

Expect to Spend

note cards	2.99
stickers	1.29
card stock	.59
Total	**$4.87**

UNDER $5!

*S*end your Yuletide wishes on special greeting cards you make yourself — for less than $5. Blank note cards and envelopes are transformed into gift-shop-quality stationery using holiday stickers along with materials you probably already have at home, such as fabric scraps, buttons, and raffia.

WHAT TO BUY
4" x 5" note cards with envelopes, package of assorted holiday stickers, and a sheet of colored card stock

THINGS YOU HAVE AT HOME
Scraps of fabric, white and decorative paper, corrugated cardboard, paper-backed fusible web, and raffia; decorative-edge craft scissors; tracing paper; assorted buttons; black permanent fine-point pen; drawing compass; and a hot glue gun

HANDMADE CHRISTMAS CARDS

Refer to photo and use the following suggestions to decorate cards.

1. Use craft scissors to cut borders or frames from card stock.

2. Refer to *Making Appliqués*, page 122, and use fabric and patterns, page 109, to make appliqués. Fuse in place on cards.

3. Use raffia bows, stickers, and written messages to decorate cards as desired.

61

CHRISTMAS KISSES

*T*he wearer of this merry cap will always be standing beneath the mistletoe at just the right moment! You can embellish a plain fleece hat with felt appliqués and simple stitches for practically nothing.

WHAT TO BUY
Fleece hat with folded brim, green felt piece, and white embroidery floss

THINGS YOU HAVE AT HOME
Tracing paper, embroidery needle, thread, and eight assorted white buttons

MISTLETOE HAT
Refer to Embroidery Stitches, page 124, before beginning project. Use six strands of floss for all stitching.

1. Trace patterns, page 97, onto tracing paper. Using patterns, cut three large leaves and four small leaves from felt.

2. Unfold brim of hat; turn hat wrong side out. With open end of hat at top, pin KISS ME!! pattern to brim of hat. Work Back Stitch and French Knots through pattern; carefully tear away pattern.

3. Turn hat right side out; refold brim. Sew mistletoe leaves and buttons to top and brim of hat.

HAPPY HOLIDAYS!

Expect to Spend

sweatshirt	5.97
waste canvas	1.30
embroidery floss	1.20
Total	**$8.47**

*K*eep a friend "in stitches" this Christmas with our festive sweatshirt. Using only five colors of embroidery floss, you can cross stitch the design over waste canvas in no time. The merry message will please someone special — and be kind to your budget, too.

WHAT TO BUY

Adult-size white sweatshirt, 1/4 yd. of 8.5 mesh waste canvas, and embroidery floss (see color key, page 104)

THINGS YOU HAVE AT HOME

Lightweight interfacing, embroidery needle, masking tape, thread, tweezers, and a spray bottle filled with water

HOLIDAY SWEATSHIRT

Refer to Cross Stitch, page 125, before beginning project.

1. Cut 9" squares from interfacing and waste canvas; baste in place on sweatshirt front.

2. Referring to chart and color key, page 104, work design over waste canvas, using six strands of floss for Cross Stitch, four strands for French Knots, and two strands for Backstitch.

3. Remove waste canvas.

COUNTRY LIGHTS

*T*hese cute country candles are just right for sharing Christmas joy! It's a snap to sponge-paint simple designs onto clay pots and then fill them with wax. Give them singly or as a set.

WHAT TO BUY
Two 3½" dia. clay pots; white, gold, red, and green acrylic paint; 2 lbs. of paraffin; and a package of wax-coated wicks

THINGS YOU HAVE AT HOME
Paintbrush, tracing paper, compressed craft sponge, natural sponge, clear acrylic spray sealer, aluminum foil, newspaper, saucepan, large can, craft stick, and a hot glue gun

FLOWERPOT CANDLES
Allow paint to dry after each color application.

1. Paint each pot with two coats of white paint.

2. Trace patterns, page 110, onto tracing paper; cut out. Draw around pattern on compressed sponge; cut out.

3. Follow *Painting Basics,* page 122, to stamp designs around each pot.

4. Use natural sponge to paint rim of each pot.

5. For tree decorations, use end of paintbrush handle to paint dots.

6. Spray each pot with sealer. Glue aluminum foil inside bottom of each pot to cover hole.

7. To make candles, follow *Making Poured Candles,* page 123, and pour melted wax into pots.

RUSTIC ACCESSORIES

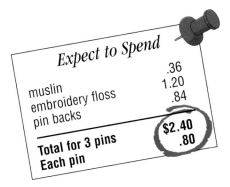
*S*end a sentimental someone on a trip back to days of old with these primitive muslin pins. Schoolgirl-style embroidery stitches create the colorful designs and rustic trims. The aged appearance is achieved using brewed coffee and a quick brush of cinnamon.

WHAT TO BUY

1/4 yd. of muslin; gold, orange, red, green, brown, and black embroidery floss; and three pin backs

THINGS YOU HAVE AT HOME

Tracing paper, transfer paper, embroidery needle, polyester fiberfill, instant coffee, ground cinnamon, and a hot glue gun

PRIMITIVE PINS

Refer to Embroidery Stitches, page 124, before beginning project. Use three strands of floss for all stitching.

Oval Pin

1. Cut two 3" x 4" rectangles from muslin.
2. Trace pattern, page 105, onto tracing paper. Follow *Making Patterns,* page 122, to transfer design onto one muslin rectangle.
3. Using gold, red, and green floss, work Backstitch over design on pin front.
4. Cut out shape along drawn line. Position shape right side down on remaining muslin rectangle. Sew 1/4" from

edge of shape. Trim edges to match pin front; clip curves.
5. Cut a 1" opening in back of pin; turn right side out. Stuff with fiberfill and whipstitch opening closed.
6. Using brown embroidery floss, work Blanket Stitch around edge of pin.
7. Brew two teaspoons of coffee in one cup of boiling water. Soak pin in coffee until desired effect is achieved; allow to cool. Squeeze out excess liquid. While pin is still wet, brush lightly with cinnamon; allow to dry.
8. Glue pin back to pin.

(Continued on page 95)

REINDEER DREAMS

A youngster will happily drift off to dreamland on Christmas Eve with a pillowcase embellished with folk-art appliqués. You can make two for just $7!

WHAT TO BUY

Two percale pillowcases and ¹/₈ yd. each of red and green fabric

THINGS YOU HAVE AT HOME

Paper-backed fusible web, scraps of assorted fabrics, pinking shears, ³/₄"w paper-backed fusible web tape, clear nylon thread, six assorted buttons, red embroidery floss, and a black permanent fine-point marker

REINDEER PILLOWCASES

1. Following *Making Appliqués*, page 122, use fabric scraps to make reindeer, nose, antler, collar, holly, berry, and star appliqués. Use pinking shears to cut three 2¹/₂" square appliqués. Arrange appliqués on pillowcase; fuse in place.

2. Use pinking shears to cut a ³/₄" x 40" strip from green fabric and a 1³/₄" x 40" strip from red fabric. Fuse web tape to back of strips. Center green strip on right side of red strip; fuse in place. Center strips over hem seam of pillowcase; fuse in place.

3. Follow *Stitching Appliqués*, page 122, to stitch around all appliqués and strips.

4. Knotting at front of button and leaving ¹/₂" tails, use floss to sew a button to center of each star.

5. Use marker to draw reindeer eyes and eyebrows.

66

DOILY DEER

Get a youngster in gear for some great Christmastime fun with this cheerful reindeer T-shirt! Plaid ribbon trims the sleeves and creates a bow tie for the whimsical doily reindeer.

WHAT TO BUY

6" dia. ecru Battenberg doily, 6" dia. ecru crocheted doily, child-size red T-shirt, 1 yd. of 1"w plaid wired ribbon, and ⁵/₈" dia. jingle bells (package of seven)

THINGS YOU HAVE AT HOME

Aluminum foil, paper-backed fusible web, scraps of white and black felt, clear nylon thread, and a safety pin

REINDEER T-SHIRT

1. For reindeer antlers, cut two 3"w shapes from Battenberg doily. Place foil over ironing board. Place doily and antler shapes, wrong side up, on foil. Place web paper side up over doilies; press. Peel doilies from foil; trim excess web. Remove paper backing and fuse doilies in place on shirt.

2. Following *Making Appliqués*, page 122, use patterns, page 108, to make eye, pupil, and nose and mouth appliqués from felt.

3. Arrange appliqués on crocheted doily, overlapping as necessary; fuse in place.

4. Refer to *Stitching Appliqués*, page 122, to sew doilies and appliqués in place.

5. Measure around each sleeve; add 1". Cut a length of ribbon the determined measurement. Press each short end ¹/₂" to wrong side. Topstitch long edges of ribbon to cuff of each sleeve.

6. Tie remaining ribbon into a bow. Sew a bell to knot of bow; pin bow to shirt. Sew three bells to neck ribbing of shirt.

GREAT GIFT BAGS

Expect to Spend

yarn	7.96
plastic canvas	.99
embroidery floss	.40
ribbon	1.00
tissue	.50
Total for 5 bags	**$10.85**
Each bag	**2.17**

*F*or a truly festive presentation, pack your gifts in these economical bags embellished with plastic canvas needlework. Whether you choose the Santa, snowman, or tree — or all three — these whimsical totes will make your gifts doubly delightful!

WHAT TO BUY

White, flesh, pink, red, blue, light green, green, and grey 3-ply sport-weight yarn; three 10" x 13" sheets of 10 mesh plastic canvas; red and green embroidery floss; red and green curling ribbon; and tissue paper

THINGS YOU HAVE AT HOME

#16 tapestry needle, black yarn, and a hot glue gun

PLASTIC CANVAS GIFT BAGS

Refer to Plastic Canvas, page 125, before beginning project.

1. For Santa ornament, cut a piece of plastic canvas measuring 28 x 31 threads. To stitch design, refer to chart and color key, page 105.

2. For Christmas tree ornament, cut a piece of plastic canvas measuring 28 x 32 threads. To stitch design, refer to chart and color key, page 103.

3. For snowman ornament, cut a piece of plastic canvas measuring 28 x 31 threads. To stitch design, refer to chart and color key, page 103.

4. For front and back of each gift bag, cut two pieces of plastic canvas measuring 44 x 48 threads. For sides, cut two pieces of plastic canvas measuring 22 x 48 threads. For handle, cut a piece of plastic canvas measuring 8 x 107 threads. For

bottom, cut one piece of plastic canvas measuring 22 x 44 threads. Use white yarn for all joining.

5. Center one ornament on front of bag and glue in place.

6. Place tissue in bag. Cut 30" lengths of red and green curling ribbon; place together and tie into a bow around handle.

68

MERRY BABY BIBS

UNDER $5!

Keep baby's dinnertime finery looking its best with our merry bibs. They're easy to make from purchased appliquéd guest towels, and at less than $3 each, the price is right!

WHAT TO BUY
Two 11" x 17" appliquéd Christmas guest towels, double fold bias tape, and $1/2$" dia. hook and loop fasteners (package of six)

THINGS YOU HAVE AT HOME
Tracing paper, fabric marker, and thread

CHRISTMAS BABY BIBS

1. Trace neck opening pattern, page 108, onto tracing paper; cut out. Use fabric marker to draw around pattern on ends of towels opposite design; cut out.

2. Follow manufacturer's instructions to bind neck openings with bias tape.

3. Sew hook and loop fasteners on bibs.

CHRISTMAS IS COOL!

All in a row, friendly snowman faces trim this spirited sweatshirt that's just right for kids. Plaid fabric around the edge of the shirt creates "scarves" for the chilly guys, and a festive message wishes a "cool" Yule!

WHAT TO BUY

Blue sweatshirt (we used a child's size large), $1/4$ yd. of plaid fabric, white and orange felt pieces, white and black embroidery floss, and $3/4$" dia. white pom-poms

THINGS YOU HAVE AT HOME

Clear nylon thread, drawing compass, tracing paper, transfer paper, and assorted black buttons

SNOWMAN SWEATSHIRT

Refer to Embroidery Stitches, page 124, before beginning project. Use three strands of floss for all stitching.

1. Cut ribbing from bottom of sweatshirt. Measure around bottom of shirt; add $1^{1}/2$". Cut a strip of fabric $2^{1}/4$" by the determined measurement.

2. Press short edges and one long edge of strip $1/2$" to wrong side. Aligning raw edges, place right side of fabric strip on wrong side of shirt. Overlapping ends as necessary; pin in place. Use a $1/4$"w seam allowance to sew strip to shirt. Turn strip to right side of shirt; press. Topstitch long folded edge of strip to shirt.

3. For snowman head pattern, use compass to draw a 4" dia. circle on tracing paper. Using pattern, cut four heads from white felt; baste in place on shirt front. Follow *Stitching Appliqués*, page 122, to stitch heads in place.

4. Referring to *Making Patterns*, page 122, trace patterns, page 96, onto tracing paper. Transfer words onto shirt and smile to each snowman head.

5. Using white floss, work Running Stitch and French Knots for words and snowflakes. Sew pom-poms to shirt.

6. Use pattern to cut four noses from orange felt. Sew one nose to each snowman head. Sew buttons to heads for eyes. Use black floss to work smiles using Running Stitch and Cross Stitch.

7. For scarves, cut four $1^{1}/4$" x 9" strips of fabric. Tie a knot in the center of each strip. Sew knot of one scarf beside each snowman.

DIMENSIONAL PORTRAIT

You won't believe how easy (and inexpensive) it is to create a gift-shop-quality accent like this one by simply layering Christmas card cutouts! The result is a unique 3-D portrait that comes to life before your eyes.

WHAT TO BUY
Box of Christmas cards with three alike, 4" x 5" piece of foam core board, poster board, 8" x 10" mat with precut opening to accommodate card, and an 8" x 10" frame with glass

THINGS YOU HAVE AT HOME
Craft glue

3-D CHRISTMAS PICTURE

1. For layers, cut desired shapes from two cards.

2. Cut small pieces from foam core board. Glue pieces onto back of each shape; glue shapes in layers onto remaining whole card.

3. Draw around outside of frame on poster board. Cut out 1/8" inside drawn line.

4. Center 3-D card on poster board piece; glue in place.

5. Insert mat behind glass; secure by bending frame staples over mat. Glue poster board with card to back of frame.

FRIENDSHIP SAMPLER

*T*his handmade sampler reminds us all of the special times that accompany the Christmas season. Bordered with a patchwork of fabric scraps and merry cutouts, the embroidered message is sure to delight a dear friend.

WHAT TO BUY

¹/₂ yd. of muslin; red, green, and brown embroidery floss; and an 11" x 14" frame

THINGS YOU HAVE AT HOME

Fabric marking pencil, paper-backed fusible web, scraps of assorted fabrics, tracing paper, craft knife, heavyweight cardboard, and a hot glue gun

CHRISTMAS SAMPLER

Refer to Embroidery Stitches, page 124, before beginning project. Use two strands of floss for all stitching.

1. For sampler background, cut two 13" x 16" pieces from muslin. Use marking pencil to draw a 9" x 11" rectangle in center of one background piece. Place background pieces together; pin in place.

2. For patchwork border, follow *Making Appliqués*, page 122, and make various lengths of 1"w rectangle appliqués from fabric scraps. Align appliqués outside drawn lines of rectangle on background piece; fuse in place.

3. Trace pattern for sampler, page 115, onto tracing paper. Center pattern inside fused border; pin in place. Stitching through pattern, use Backstitch, French Knots, Stem Stitch, and Running Stitch to embroider design on sampler. Carefully tear away pattern.

4. Use patterns, page 115, and remaining fabric scraps to make tree, star, heart, gingerbread man, circle, and present appliqués. Arrange appliqués around saying; fuse in place.

5. Use craft knife to cut an 11" x 14" piece of cardboard. Center sampler on cardboard, wrapping edges to back; glue in place. Glue sampler to back of frame.

Expect to Spend

craft storage box	3.99
paint	1.27
fabric	1.99
cord	1.99
Total	**$9.24**

This clever keeper offers a friend an elegant place to tuck away holiday memories. Our handsome memory box features a padded lid accented with a lattice of golden cord. The roomy box can hold snapshots, mementos, and more!

WHAT TO BUY

7¹/₂" x 11" red craft storage box, gold acrylic paint, ¹/₂ yd. of Christmas print fabric, and gold cord (9-ft spool)

THINGS YOU HAVE AT HOME

Natural sponge, batting, four buttons, pushpin, clear nylon thread, and a hot glue gun

MEMORY BOX

1. Referring to *Painting Basics,* page 122, use gold paint to sponge paint box bottom; allow to dry.

2. Cut an 11¹/₂" x 15" rectangle from batting. Cut a 1¹/₂" square from each corner. Glue batting to top and sides of box lid.

(Continued on page 92)

"SPEC-TACULAR" GIFT

*I*magine the delight in someone's eyes when you deliver this sweet surprise — Mrs. Claus all decked out in wire spectacles and a nightcap made from a doily. Fill her with treats for a "spec-tacular" gift!

WHAT TO BUY

4" dia. glass ivy bowl, two 5.5-oz. bags of candy, 9$^{1}/_{2}$" dia. doily, $^{2}/_{3}$ yd. of $^{1}/_{4}$"w red ribbon, 15mm wiggle eyes, red craft foam, white curly craft hair, and one pair of 3$^{1}/_{2}$"w doll glasses

THINGS YOU HAVE AT HOME

Poster board, polyester fiberfill, rubber band, tracing paper, and craft glue

MRS. SANTA CANDY DISH

1. Draw around rim of bowl on poster board; cut out.

2. Place candy in bowl. Glue a ball of fiberfill to poster board circle. Place circle fiberfill side up on bowl.

3. For hat, center doily over fiberfill; secure around rim of bowl with rubber band. Tie ribbon into a bow around rim, covering rubber band.

4. Trace pattern, page 102, onto tracing paper; cut out. Using pattern, cut one mouth from craft foam. Glue eyes and mouth to bowl; glue hair to bowl under rim of hat.

5. Hook temples of glasses into lace of doily to hold in place over eyes.

74

WANTED: ONE JOLLY ELF!

Expect to Spend

chalkboard	1.97
paint	2.91
craft foam	2.37
jingle bell	.50
magnetic strip	.97
Total	**$8.72**

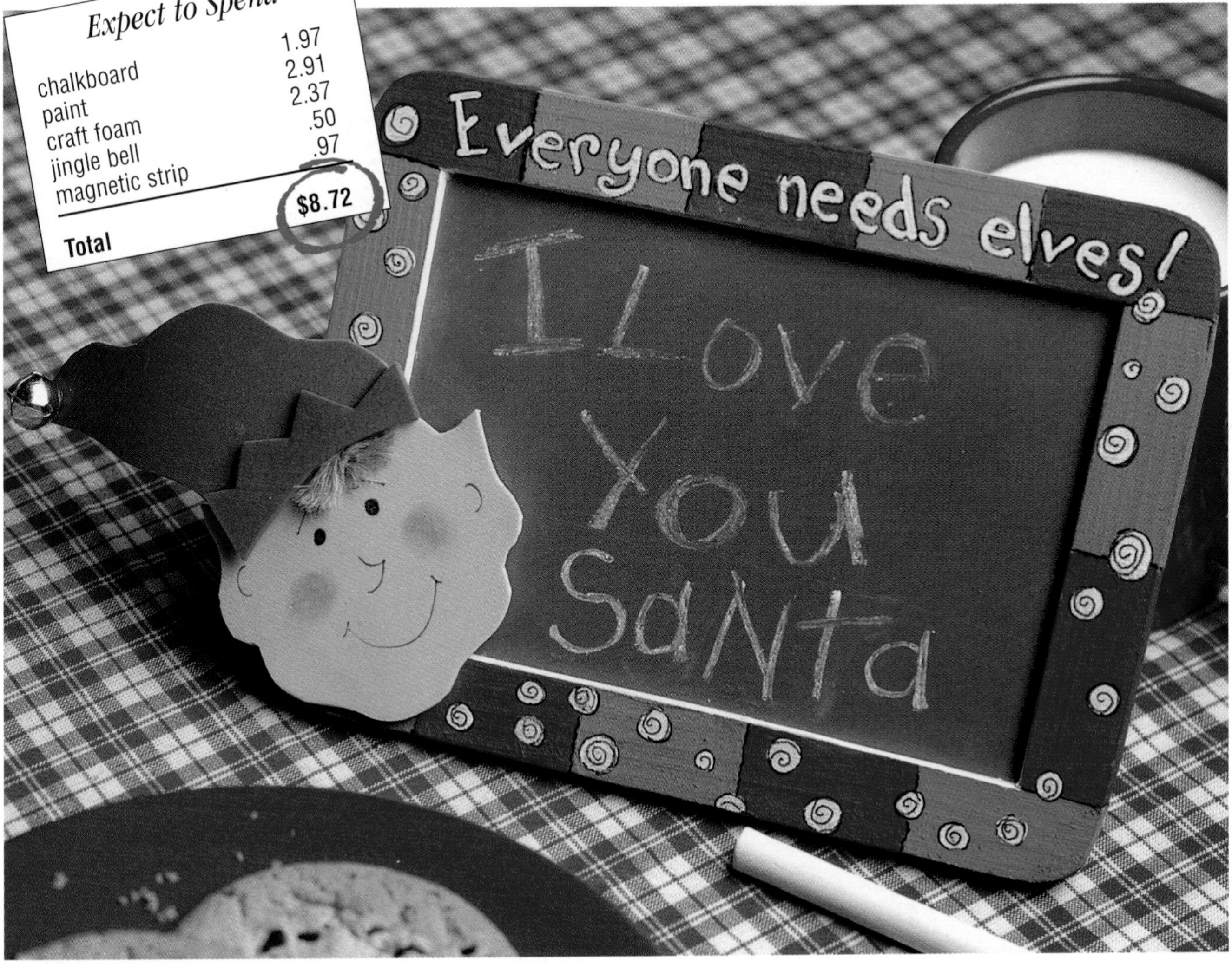

This jolly little elf is "slated" for stardom! Using craft foam and paints, you can transform an inexpensive chalkboard into a cherished holiday gift for a youngster.

WHAT TO BUY

$5\frac{5}{8}$" x $7\frac{5}{8}$" chalkboard with wooden frame; white, red, and green acrylic paint; peach, red, and green craft foam; $\frac{1}{2}$" dia. jingle bell; and a roll of $\frac{1}{2}$"w self-adhesive magnetic strip

THINGS YOU HAVE AT HOME

Paintbrushes, tracing paper, transfer paper, black felt-tip pen, blush for cheeks, jute twine, and a hot glue gun

ELF CHALKBOARD

Allow paint to dry after each color application.

1. Paint red and green rectangles along frame of chalkboard.

2. Trace patterns, page 96, onto tracing paper. Follow *Making Patterns,* page 122, to transfer message onto frame of chalkboard; paint words white. Paint white dots on frame. Use pen to draw around letters, draw designs on circles, and draw lines between rectangles.

(Continued on page 91)

CUSTOM GIFT BASKETS

*I*nstead of delivering your Christmas goodies in plain paper bags, transform ordinary baskets into custom carriers for your treats! Simply wrap a basket in homespun fabric, add a little padding, and tie off with jute. Holly leaves and berries cut from felt add the finishing touches.

WHAT TO BUY

5" dia. basket, ¹/₂ yd. of fabric, and red green felt pieces

THINGS YOU HAVE AT HOME

¹/₂"w paper-backed fusible web tape, rubber band, polyester fiberfill, jute rope, tracing paper, wire cutters, floral wire, thread, and a hot glue gun

FABRIC-COVERED BASKET

1. Measure basket from one side of rim to opposite side of rim (Fig. 1); multiply by 1¹/₂ and add ¹/₂" (this will be diameter of fabric circle). Cut a square of fabric 2" larger than the determined diameter.

Fig. 1

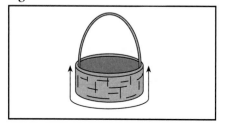

2. Follow *Cutting a Fabric Circle*, page 123, to cut a circle the determined diameter. Fuse web tape to wrong side of fabric around edge of circle. Turn edge ¹/₂" to wrong side; fuse in place.

3. Center basket on wrong side of fabric circle. Bring edges of fabric up and secure around rim of basket with rubber band; adjust gathers evenly.

4. Tuck fiberfill between fabric and sides of basket for desired fullness.

5. Tie a 25" length of jute into a knot around basket, covering rubber band. Knot ends of jute.

6. Trace patterns, page 121, onto tracing paper. Using patterns, cut four holly leaves from green felt and three berries from red felt.

7. Cut two 2¹/₂" lengths of floral wire. Glue wires along center of two leaves. Glue remaining two leaves over wired leaves. Arrange leaves as desired.

8. Hand baste along edge of each berry; pull thread to gather slightly. Insert a small amount of fiberfill inside berry; pull thread tightly to gather around fiberfill. Knot and trim thread ends.

9. Glue leaves and berries over jute knot.

REINDEER DREAM TEAM

UNDER $5!

*E*ven Santa couldn't beat these whimsical gift sacks! They're just the thing for bagging up small gifts for neighbors or co-workers. And at a cost of only 44¢ each, you can craft a whole team of reindeer.

WHAT TO BUY
Brown paper lunch bags (package of 50), three packages of 15mm oval wiggle eyes (three pair per package), three packages of 1½" dia. pom-poms (three per package), and brown chenille stems

THINGS YOU HAVE AT HOME
Drawing compass, jute twine, scraps of fabric, and a hot glue gun

REINDEER GIFT BAGS
1. For each bag, fold top 3½" of bag to front. Use compass to draw a 6" dia. half-circle on folded end of bag; cut along drawn line.

2. Cut a 4¼" length of jute; unravel slightly. Glue jute to fold of bag.

3. Cut a ½" x 5" strip of fabric; tie into a bow. Glue bow to center of jute.

4. For face, glue eyes and pom-pom to bag.

5. Cut six 6" lengths of chenille stems. For each antler, twist two lengths around center of one length of chenille stem.

Glue one end of each antler to inside top of bag.

77

Trim THE TREE

Spice up your ornament collection with exciting new tree-trimmers! Your evergreen will command attention when you add one-of-a-kind decorations like jolly old elves, whimsical paintbrush Santas, or glowing snowman light covers. So don't spend extra money on those department-store trims — come craft with us!

UNDER $5!

*W*arm and toasty, our mini mitten ornaments will add a wintry feel to your evergreen. Fused-on fabric scraps are used to create the folksy designs, which are accented with hand-stitched messages to complete the homestyle look.

WHAT TO BUY
Pair of miniature mittens and red embroidery floss

THINGS YOU HAVE AT HOME
Scraps of assorted fabrics, paper-backed fusible web, and a black permanent fine-point pen

MINI MITTEN ORNAMENTS
1. Follow *Making Appliqués*, page 122, and use patterns, page 106, to make tree, heart, star, leaf, and trunk appliqués from fabric scraps.

2. Arrange appliqués on mittens; fuse in place. Use pen to draw detail lines on leaves.

3. Use three strands of floss and work Backstitch, page 124, to stitch "Love" on one mitten cuff and "Joy" on remaining mitten cuff.

PEACEFUL TIDINGS

Who *better than an angel to watch over your family and friends? This country-style seraph begins as a wooden spoon, and delicate tea-dyed doilies provide her easy-to-make apron and wings. For a heavenly price, she'll spread peace to all who enter your holiday home.*

WHAT TO BUY

17" long wooden spoon, two 12" dia. doilies, 1/3 yd. of muslin, 1/8"w green ribbon (10-yd. spool), 1/4"w ecru ribbon (10-yd. spool), wool doll hair, and a sprig of artificial holly

THINGS YOU HAVE AT HOME

Two tea bags, five 5/8" dia. buttons, black fine-point pen, red colored pencil, rubber band, 1" dia. button, string, and a hot glue gun

HOMESPUN ANGEL

1. Steep tea in two cups of boiling water and allow to cool. Soak doilies in tea until desired shade is achieved; allow to dry. Press doilies.

2. For dress, tear a 12 1/2" x 17" rectangle from muslin. Spacing 4" apart, glue 5/8" dia. buttons along one long edge

(Continued on page 93)

81

SNOWMAN LUMINARIES

These adorable ornaments will receive glowing remarks when you hang them on the evergreen! Illuminated by miniature Christmas lights, the chilly weather guys are created from sponge-painted jars. A ladies' knit glove provides a cuddly hat for each ornament.

WHAT TO BUY
Package of bamboo skewers and a pair of ladies' knit gloves

THINGS YOU HAVE AT HOME
Two small jars with lids; large nail; hammer; natural sponge; white, orange, and black acrylic paint; small stencil brush; small paintbrush; needle; thread; green yarn; clear nylon thread; scrap of plaid fabric; four white buttons; dried greenery; and a hot glue gun

LUMINOUS SNOWMAN ORNAMENTS

Allow paint to dry after each application.

1. For each ornament, remove lid from jar. Use hammer and nail to make a hole in center of lid large enough for miniature Christmas light. Replace lid on jar.

2. Follow *Painting Basics*, page 122, and use white paint to sponge paint outside of jar. Use stencil brush to paint snowman eyes and mouth black. For nose, cut a 1"

length from one end of skewer; paint orange. Glue nose to jar. Paint glue white.

3. For hat, cut fingers and thumb from one glove. Leaving thumb opening for inserting light, hand baste around top of glove; pull threads to gather. Tie thread ends and clip. Referring to *Making a Pom-pom*, page 123, use yarn to make a pom-pom. Sew pom-pom to gathers of hat.

4. For hanger, thread ends of a 10" length of nylon thread through pom-pom and top of hat; knot ends together. Roll up cuff of hat. Positioning light opening at back of ornament, glue hat around top of jar.

5. For scarf, tear a $3/4$" x 14" strip of fabric; tie strip around bottom of jar. Glue buttons to scarf and hat. Glue greenery to hat.

6. To light ornament, hang on tree and insert miniature bulb from Christmas lights through holes in hat and jar.

PAINTBRUSH PALS

UNDER $5!

*W*himsical felt faces add pleasing personality to our clever Santa ornaments. You can make three of these jolly paintbrush pals for less than $3 each. They make great offerings for friends and neighbors!

WHAT TO BUY
Three 2¹/₂" x 8¹/₂" paintbrushes; one white, one ecru, one pink, one black, and two red felt pieces; black embroidery floss; ¹/₈ yd. of artificial lamb's wool; and three 1" dia. pom-poms

THINGS YOU HAVE AT HOME
Tracing paper, pinking shears, white acrylic paint, small paintbrush, thread, and a hot glue gun

PAINTBRUSH SANTAS
1. Trace patterns, page 103, onto tracing paper. For each Santa, use patterns to cut eyes from white felt, irises from black felt, and cheeks, nose, and chin from pink felt. Use pinking shears to cut head shape from ecru felt. Arrange face pieces on head; glue in place.

2. For highlights, apply a dot of white paint on each eye and nose.

(Continued on page 93)

COUNTRY ANGELS

UNDER $5!

*S*pread glad tidings with these charming country angels. There's no sewing involved, and it's a heavenly way to "recycle" brown paper bags! At less than 50¢ apiece, these ornaments are also great treats for co-workers.

WHAT TO BUY
$^1/_8$ yd. of fabric and $^1/_3$ yd. of $^1/_8$"w ribbon

THINGS YOU HAVE AT HOME
Paper-backed fusible web, scraps of assorted fabric, brown paper bag, black permanent felt-tip pen, pink colored pencil, facial tissues, natural raffia, scraps of red embroidery floss, wire cutters, craft wire, clear nylon thread, and craft glue

PAPER BAG ANGEL ORNAMENTS
1. Follow *Making Appliqués*, page 122, and use patterns, page 107, to make angel A, angel B, and two 1" square patch appliqués from fabric and fabric scraps.

2. For each ornament, cut two 6" x 9" rectangles from paper bag. Arrange appliqués on one rectangle; fuse in place. Cut $^1/_4$" outside edge of appliqués.

3. Use pen to draw "stitches" around collar, patch, and border of ornament and to draw eyes and mouth. Use pink pencil to color cheeks.

4. For back of each ornament, draw around ornament front on remaining paper rectangle; cut out. Leaving an opening for stuffing, glue front and back ornament edges together. Stuff ornament lightly with tissues; glue opening closed.

5. For hair, cut several 4" lengths of raffia; knot ends together with embroidery floss; glue hair to angel's head. Cut a 3" length of embroidery floss; tie into a bow. Glue bow to collar.

6. For halo, cut a 5" length of craft wire and bend into an oval shape; twist ends together and glue above hair.

7. For hanger, fold a 6" length of thread in half and knot ends together; glue to back of ornament.

STELLAR ORNAMENTS

*N*ow there's a way to display all your holiday "stars" on the Christmas tree! For a few dollars and just a little time, you can make a galaxy of stellar photo ornaments.

WHAT TO BUY
Five 3³/₄"w plastic star ornaments, gold spray paint, ¹/₈ yd. of Christmas print fabric, and ¹/₈"w red satin ribbon (10-yd. spool)

THINGS YOU HAVE AT HOME
Poster board, paper-backed fusible web, photographs, ¹/₈" dia. hole punch, and craft glue

STAR PHOTO ORNAMENTS
1. Paint each ornament; allow to dry.

2. Cut two 4¹/₄" x 24" rectangles each from fabric and fusible web and one from poster board. Follow web manufacturer's instructions to fuse fabric to both sides of poster board. Draw around star ornament five times on fabric-covered poster board. Cut out each shape just inside drawn line.

3. Draw around fused star shape on desired photographs; cut out ¹/₄" inside drawn line. Center photograph on one side of fabric star and glue in place. Punch a hole in top point of star.

4. Cut five 8" and five 15" lengths of ribbon. For each ornament hanger, thread one 15" ribbon through hole in star and ornament; knot close to ornament. Knot ends of streamers together. Tie one 8" ribbon into a bow around each hanger.

JOLLY OLD ELF

UNDER $5!

Let St. Nick's jolly mug brighten your tree! The padded ornament is easy to make from felt and embellish with a raffia beard. Craft a pair for less than $4 — you can keep them both for yourself or share with a friend.

WHAT TO BUY

Ecru felt piece, brown embroidery floss, $1/4$" dia. jingle bell, $1/16$"w green ribbon (10-yd. spool), and natural raffia

THINGS YOU HAVE AT HOME

Tracing paper, scraps of pink and red fabrics, drawing compass, pinking shears, polyester fiberfill, and a hot glue gun

SANTA FACE ORNAMENTS

Refer to Embroidery Stitches, page 124, before beginning project. Use six strands of floss for all stitching.

1. Trace patterns, page 110, onto tracing paper. For each ornament, use patterns to cut one nose and two cheeks from pink fabric. Fold cheek pattern in half; use to cut one mouth from red fabric.

2. For head/hat pattern, use compass to draw a $4^1/4$" dia. circle on tracing paper. Use pattern and pinking shears to cut two heads from felt and one hat from red fabric.

3. Using embroidery floss, work long Straight Stitches to sew cheeks and nose on one head shape. Work French Knots for eyes. Glue mouth on face.

4. Matching wrong sides and leaving an opening for stuffing, use floss to whipstitch head pieces together. Stuff with fiberfill; sew opening closed.

5. For hat, fold red $4^1/2$" circle in half. Insert 1" of head between layers at fold; glue in place. For point, fold remainder of hat to front; glue in place. Tie a 4" length of ribbon into a bow; glue bow and a jingle bell to point of hat.

6. For beard and mustache, cut several 8" lengths of raffia. Place lengths together and knot in center. Repeat to make six bundles. Glue one bundle under nose for mustache, and five bundles along bottom of mouth for beard.

7. For hanger, cut a 6" length of clear nylon thread; knot ends and sew to back of ornament.

FOLK-ART MITTENS

UNDER $5!

*A*dd a toasty touch to the evergreen with cozy corduroy mittens. These folksy ornaments are appliquéd with felt flowers and trimmed in blanket stitching for a country look. You can make a handful of them for less than $6!

WHAT TO BUY
¹/₂ yd. each of red corduroy and heavy-weight fusible interfacing; one gold, one green, and three white felt pieces; green embroidery floss; and ³/₈"w red satin ribbon (10-yd. spool)

THINGS YOU HAVE AT HOME
Tracing paper, paper-backed fusible web, embroidery needle, pinking shears, buttons, and craft glue

MITTEN ORNAMENTS
1. Follow manufacturer's instructions to fuse interfacing to wrong side of corduroy.

2. Trace pattern, page 99, onto tracing paper. Using pattern, cut two mitten shapes (one in reverse) for each ornament from corduroy.

3. Referring to *Making Appliqués,* page 122, use patterns, page 99, to make flower and flower center appliqués from felt. Fuse flower center appliqué on flower.

4. Using three strands of floss, work Blanket Stitch, page 124, around edge of flower. Arrange appliqués on right side of one mitten shape; fuse in place. Sew a button to flower center.

5. Matching wrong sides, place mitten front and back together; pin in place. Use Blanket Stitch to sew mitten pieces together, leaving top edge open.

6. For cuff, use pinking shears to cut a 3" x 7" rectangle from white felt. Overlapping short ends at back, glue cuff to top of mitten; allow to dry. Fold cuff over top of mitten.

7. For hanger, cut a 6" length of ribbon. Fold ribbon in half and sew ends to inside top edge of cuff.

ELFIN MAGIC

*A*dd a little elfin magic to the season with this whimsical ornament! He's fashioned from print fabrics and felt pieces, and a chenille twist candy cane serves as a cute hanger. You can craft him for less than $4!

WHAT TO BUY

Flesh, red, green, and black felt pieces; red and white striped chenille twists; 1/4" dia. red pom-poms; and a 6mm jingle bell

THINGS YOU HAVE AT HOME

Tracing paper, scraps of Christmas print fabrics, utility scissors, jute twine, scrap of black embroidery floss, and a hot glue gun

ELF ORNAMENT

1. Trace patterns, page 109, onto tracing paper; cut out. Using patterns, cut one hat, one collar, two heads, four hands, and two feet from felt pieces and two shirts from fabric.

2. For arms, cut two 3/4" x 12" strips of fabric. Center a chenille twist along wrong side of one arm strip; glue in place. Matching wrong sides and long edges, glue arm strips together; use utility scissors to cut in half. Glue one end of each arm between two hands. Glue remaining ends at an angle between shoulders on wrong side of shirt back.

3. For legs, cut two 1/2" x 6" strips of fabric. Matching wrong sides, glue legs together; cut in half. Glue one end of each leg to wrong side of shirt back along bottom edge; glue feet to remaining ends of legs. Matching wrong sides, glue shirt front to shirt back.

4. Glue head shapes together. For hair, cut a 2" length of twine; untwist slightly. Glue hair and hat on head. Fold top of hat over and glue in place. Glue head and collar to shirt.

5. Bend arms to make "elbows" and make hands meet over elf's head. Cut a 6" length from chenille twist; bend into a candy cane shape. Glue candy cane between hands.

6. Glue one pom-pom to each toe and one to face for nose. For mouth, cut a 1 1/2" length of floss; glue one strand to face. Glue jingle bell to tip of hat.

A TOUCH OF NOSTALGIA

Expect to Spend

felt	.80
Total	**$.80**

UNDER $5!

*B*ring a touch of nostalgia to the tree with this charming heart, or select brighter shades of felt for a modern look. At only 80¢ apiece, the pockets would also make nice little gifts or party favors — just fill them with peppermint sticks or other treats.

WHAT TO BUY
Ecru, red, green, and dark green felt pieces

THINGS YOU HAVE AT HOME
Pinking shears, paper-backed fusible web, black embroidery floss, and six assorted small and large white buttons

HEART POCKET ORNAMENT

Refer to Embroidery Stitches, page 124, before beginning project. Use three strands of floss for all stitching.

1. For hanger, use pinking shears to cut a ¹/₂" x 8¹/₂" strip from dark green felt piece; set aside. Matching short edges, fold and cut all felt pieces in half.

2. Follow *Making Appliqués,* page 122, and use patterns, page 114, to make heart and leaf appliqués. For each side of ornament, use pinking shears to cut small heart appliqué from red felt. Cut large heart appliqué from dark green felt. Center red heart on green heart; fuse in place. Position fused hearts on one ecru felt piece; fuse in place. Use pinking shears to cut out ecru heart ¹/₈" from edge of green heart.

3. Sew ends of hanger to wrong sides of hearts as indicated in Fig. 1.

Fig. 1

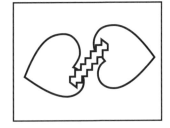

4. For flower, stack one small button on larger button; use floss to sew in place on red heart. Arrange leaf appliqués near flower; fuse in place.

5. Covering hanger stitching, sew remaining buttons onto front and back of ornament.

6. Matching wrong sides and leaving top edges of pocket open, work Running Stitch around edges to sew hearts together.

SUPER SNOWFLAKES

*H*ere's a super project idea to share with a friend — adorable snowflake snowmen ornaments. You can make two for less than $6, so keep one for yourself and give the other to a favorite pal!

WHAT TO BUY

2" dia. plastic foam ball, Aleene's True Snow™, 5mm black flat-back beads, black craft foam, 1/3 yd. of 7/8"w plaid ribbon, and two 5" dia. acrylic snowflake ornaments

THINGS YOU HAVE AT HOME

Serrated knife, plastic sandwich bag, paintbrush, white and orange acrylic paint, tracing paper, drawing compass, cardboard tube from paper towels, and a hot glue gun

SNOWFLAKE SNOWMEN

1. Use knife to cut foam ball in half. Follow manufacturer's instructions to apply snow to rounded side of each half; allow to dry.

2. For nose, place a small amount of artificial snow in corner of plastic bag. Cut tip from corner of bag. Squeeze nose shape onto each snowman face; allow to dry. Paint noses orange.

3. Glue five beads to each face for mouth. Trace pattern, page 100, onto tracing paper. Using pattern, cut four eyes from craft foam. Paint a white dot in each eye. Glue eyes to each face.

4. For hats, use compass to draw a 2 1/2" dia. circle on craft foam; cut out. Cut a 1" long section from cardboard tube. Position tube section cut side down at center of foam circle; draw around outside. Cut foam circle and tube piece in half. Cut inner half-circle from each foam circle half. Measure tube piece; cut two pieces of craft foam the determined measurement. Glue foam pieces to outside of each tube piece. Glue each hat brim and tube piece together. Glue one inner half-circle to top of each hat.

5. Glue one snowman head to center of each snowflake.

6. For scarves, cut ribbon in half; tie a knot in center of each half. Glue one scarf to bottom of each snowman head.

ELF CHALKBOARD
(Continued from page 75)

3. Using patterns, cut head from peach craft foam, hat from green craft foam, and hatband from red craft foam.

4. Glue hatband and bell on hat; glue hat to top of head.

5. Use pen to draw face. Apply blush to cheeks.

6. For hair, cut a 1" length of twine; fray slightly. Glue hair below hat.

7. Glue elf to chalkboard frame.

8. Adhere two 4" lengths of magnetic strip to back of chalkboard.

PILLOW COVER
(Continued from page 25)

of print napkins to front of pillow over red napkin. Working from inside, pin edges of napkins together at ends of pillow (Fig. 1).

Fig. 1

FESTIVE HOLIDAY MITTENS
(Continued from page 48)

GREEN MITTENS

1. Trace pattern, page 97, onto tracing paper; cut out. Using pattern, cut two snowmen from white felt.

2. Pin one snowman on each mitten. Using green floss, work Blanket Stitch around edge of snowman. Using black floss, work French Knots for eyes and mouth and Stem Stitch for arms. Using orange floss, work Satin Stitch for nose.

3. For snowflakes, sew six buttons to each mitten.

RED MITTENS

1. Trace patterns, page 97, onto tracing paper; cut out. Using patterns, cut trees from green felt and tree trunks from black felt. Overlapping as necessary, pin felt pieces to mittens. Using green floss, work Blanket Stitch around edges of each tree and tree trunk.

2. Use ecru floss to sew buttons to tree and mitten cuff.

CHRISTMAS KITCHEN ANGEL
(Continued from page 27)

together; turn right side out. Stuff head with fiberfill; sew opening closed.

3. For hair, cut two 24" lengths of floss. Placing lengths together, thread tapestry needle; knot 1/2" from end. Beginning at eye level on head seam, take a small stitch. Knot floss at end of stitch and cut 1/2" from knot. Repeat along seam to opposite side of head.

4. For body, tear an 11" x 12" rectangle from muslin. Center and pin message pattern to right half of rectangle. Work Running Stitch for words, stems, and leaves of flowers. Work Lazy Daisy Stitch for center flower petals and French Knots for flower center. Sew a button to top of each remaining stem.

5. Matching wrong sides, fold body in half. Insert head between layers at top of body; pin in place. Leaving an opening for stuffing, use gold floss to sew 1/2" from raw edges. Stuff body with fiberfill; sew opening closed. Sew a button below neck. Tie a 10" length of red floss into a bow around button; tie a knot at end of each streamer.

6. For arms, center 12" twig on back of angel; glue in place. Glue a small piece of cedar and bird to one arm.

7. For wings, glue cedar branches to back of angel above arms.

8. For legs, insert 2" of remaining twigs between stitches at bottom of body; glue in place.

9. For halo, cut a 6" length of twine; tie ends together, forming a loop. Glue halo to back of head.

10. For hanger, thread needle with a 4" length of floss. Take a stitch on back of head; tie ends of floss into a knot.

CORDUROY SNOWMAN STOCKING
(Continued from page 35)

6. For hanger, cut a $2^{1}/_{4}$" x 7" strip of black corduroy. Matching right sides and long edges, fold strip in half and stitch long edges together; turn right side out. Fold in half and sew ends to inside top edge of stocking.

7. For hat band, tear a 1" x 19" strip of flannel. Tie strip into a knot around hat.

8. Tear a 2" x 18" strip from flannel. Tie into a bow; sew to stocking front.

MEMORY BOX
(Continued from page 73)

3. Cut a 14" x 18" rectangle from fabric. Center box lid on wrong side of fabric rectangle. Folding in excess fabric at corners, bring fabric edges to inside of lid; glue in place.

4. Cut two 18" lengths of cord. Crossing cords diagonally over box lid, glue ends of each length to opposite corners.

5. Cut a 38" length of cord. Form cord into a diamond shape with points extending over edges of lid; center points of diamond on each side of lid and glue in place. Trim any excess cord. Glue a button over each point of cord.

6. Working from top side of lid, use pushpin to make a hole at each side of each cord intersection. Use nylon thread to stitch cord to lid, pulling thread taut and tying into a knot on wrong side of lid. Place a dot of glue over each knot.

HOLLY TREE SKIRT
(Continued from page 38)

2. Referring to *Cutting a Fabric Circle*, page 123, cut a 40" dia. circle from corduroy. Repeat to cut a 7" dia. circle from center of large circle. For opening, cut through one layer of fabric from outer to inner edge. Turn all raw edges $^{1}/_{2}$" to wrong side; press. Clip curves.

3. Fuse web tape to wrong side of turned edges of tree skirt. Remove paper backing and fuse hems in place.

4. Using three strands of floss, work Running Stitch, page 124, to sew leaves to tree skirt.

5. Using yo-yo patterns, cut nineteen of each size circle from green fabrics. Turn raw edge of each circle $^{1}/_{8}$" to wrong side. Using a double strand of thread, hand baste along turned edge. Pull threads to tightly gather circle; knot thread and trim ends. Flatten circle. Sew yo-yos to tree skirt.

HOMESPUN ANGEL
(Continued from page 81)

of dress. Use pen to write message between buttons.

3. Use pen to draw face on back of spoon. Use red pencil to color cheeks.

4. Gather dress around spoon handle; secure with rubber band. Adjust gathers evenly. For apron, fold 2½" of one doily to right side. Position apron over dress; glue in place. Cut a 26" length of each color ribbon. Tie ribbons together in a bow around top of apron. Glue 1" button over knot of bow.

5. For wings, tie a length of string tightly around center of remaining doily; adjust gathers evenly. Glue wings to back of angel.

6. Cut a 9" length of doll hair and a 3½" length of ecru ribbon. Knot ribbon around center of hair length; fluff hair slightly. Glue hair to top of angel head.

7. Remove three leaves from holly sprig. Glue one leaf over knot of hair ribbon and two leaves to front of dress.

PAINTBRUSH SANTAS
(Continued from page 83)

3. Use three strands of floss to work Straight Stitch, page 125, for eyelashes and mouth.

4. For mustache, cut an ⅛" dia. bundle of bristles from back of paintbrush. Knot thread around center of bundle; clip thread ends close to mustache. Glue mustache to head. Glue head to paintbrush.

5. For hat, use pinking shears to cut a 6" square from red felt. For hat trim, cut two ¾" x 6" strips of lamb's wool; glue to two edges of hat as shown in Fig. 1.

Fig. 1

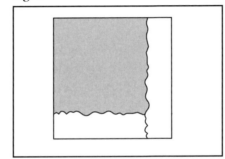

6. Position paintbrush diagonally over wrong side of hat. Wrap hat around paintbrush; glue in place.

7. Glue a pom-pom to top of hat.

FUN FELT CANVAS TOTE BAG
(Continued from page 55)

appliqués, and four cuff appliqués, using pinking shears to cut out cuffs and pom-poms. Arrange appliqués on each Santa; fuse in place.

6. Cut a 19" length of rickrack; hand sew to edge of gingerbread boy. For bow tie, cut a 6" length of red ribbon. Fold ribbon into a bow; wrap red floss around center to secure. Glue bow to gingerbread boy.

7. Sew buttons on front of each figure.

8. Measure around top of bag; add 1". Use pinking shears to cut a strip of fabric 1¼" by the determined measurement; cut a length of ½"w green ribbon the determined measurement. Center web tape on wrong side of fabric strip; fuse in place. Overlapping ends ½", fuse fabric strip to top of bag. Glue ribbon length along center of fabric strip. Center buttons on ribbon along front of bag; sew in place.

9. Use pinking shears to cut two ½" x 7" strips of fabric. Tie each strip into a bow. Cut a 19" length of ⅛"w ribbon. Leaving a 2" tail at each end, glue ribbon to center front of bag, 1¼" from each edge.

10. Spacing 1" apart, glue Santas and gingerbread boy along ribbon. Glue fabric bows between figures.

CROCHETED STOCKING
(Continued from page 43)

★ two times more, YO and draw through all four loops on hook (counts as one dc).

Rnd 3: Ch 2, dc in next dc, dc decrease, dc in next 2 dc, double decrease, dc in next 2 dc, dc decrease 4 times, dc in next 2 dc, double decrease, dc in next 2 dc, dc decrease twice; join with slip st to first dc: 18 dc.

Rnd 4: Ch 2, dc in next dc, dc decrease, dc in next dc, dc decrease 4 times, dc in next dc, dc decrease twice; join with slip st to first dc, finish off leaving a long end for sewing.

Thread yarn needle with end. Flatten Heel, keeping joining at fold, then sew seam.

CUFF
Rnd 1: With wrong side facing and working in free loops of beginning ch, join green with slip st in marked ch, do not remove marker; ch 3, dc in next ch and in each ch around; join with slip st to first dc: 48 dc.

Rnd 2-4: Ch 3, dc in next dc and in each dc around; join with slip st to first dc.

Note: To work sc decrease, pull up a loop in next two sc. YO and draw through all three loops on hook.

Rnd 5 (Points): ★ † Ch 1, sc in same st and in next 7 dc, ch 1, turn; sc decrease, sc in next 4 sc, sc decrease, ch 1, turn; sc decrease, sc in next 2 sc, sc decrease, ch 1, turn; sc decrease twice, ch 1, turn, sc decrease; slip st evenly across end of rows †, slip st in next dc on Rnd 4; repeat from ★ 4 times more, then repeat from † to † once; join with slip st in same st as first sc, finish off.

Fold Cuff to right side.

HANGER
With right side facing and working around beginning ch, join red with slip st in sp between dc to the left of marked ch, remove marker; ch 15, slip st in same sp as joining; finish off.

Thread one 9" length of ribbon through each point and bell. Tie ribbons into bows.

SNOWMAN BASKET
(Continued from page 52)

one strand of red floss and work Blanket Stitch to sew each pair of mitten shapes together. Lightly stuff each mitten with fiberfill. Glue one mitten over hand-sewn end of each arm.

5. For stocking hat, cut 5" from ribbing end of one red sock. Fold finished edge of ribbing 1" to right side. Tie jute into a bow around middle of ribbing. Glue hat to one head.

6. For nightcap, use compass to draw a 6" dia. circle pattern on tracing paper. Cut foot part of red sock open and lay flat. Using circle pattern, cut cap from sock piece; glue lace trim around edge. Baste around circle 1/2" inside edge. Pull thread ends to loosely gather cap; knot thread ends to secure. Lightly stuff cap with fiberfill. Glue cap to remaining head.

7. Matching ends of each pair of arms at ends of basket and placing arms along sides of basket, glue arms in place. Glue heads to top edge of basket where arms join.

8. For each scarf, tear a 1 1/4" x 19" piece of fabric. Loosely tie strip around base of each head.

PRIMITIVE PINS
(Continued from page 65)

Heart Pin
1. Cut two 3" x 5" rectangles from muslin.
2. Trace pattern, page 105, onto tracing paper. Follow *Making Patterns,* page 122, to transfer design onto one muslin rectangle.
3. Using orange, red, brown, and black floss, work Backstitch, Cross Stitch, and French Knots over design on pin front.
4. Follow Steps 4 - 8 of Oval Pin, page 65, to complete pin.

Star Pin
1. Cut two 4" square pieces from muslin.
2. Trace pattern, page 105, onto tracing paper. Follow *Making Patterns,* page 122, to transfer design onto one muslin rectangle.
3. Using gold, red, and green floss, work Backstitch and French Knots over design on front of pin.
4. Follow Steps 4 - 8 of Oval Pin, page 65, to complete pin.

CHRISTMAS CARD WALL HANGING
(Continued from page 39)

side. Fuse web tape to wrong sides of binding strips. Centering edges of background between folds, fuse top and bottom binding strips, then side binding strips to background.

5. For hanging sleeve, cut 4" x 35" pieces from fabric and fusible interfacing; fuse together. Press edges ¹/₂" to wrong side. Fuse a length of web tape along top and bottom edges of hanging sleeve. Position hanging sleeve on wrong side of wall hanging ¹/₄" below top edge; fuse in place.

6. Using pattern, page 120, make two gingerbread boy appliqués from tan fabric. Cut two 5¹/₂" x 7" pieces from felt. Center one gingerbread boy on each felt piece; fuse in place. Use pinking shears to trim felt ¹/₄" outside edges of gingerbread boys.

7. Using black floss, work Running Stitch to outline gingerbread boys, French Knots for eyes, and Stem Stitch for mouth. Punch two holes from red fabric scrap for cheeks for each gingerbread boy; glue in place.

8. Tear two ¹/₂" x 6" strips from fabric scraps; tie each into a bow. Glue one bow on each gingerbread boy.

9. Paint wooden heart buttons red; allow to dry. Use red embroidery floss to sew heart buttons and ³/₄" dia. buttons to gingerbread boys; glue to wall hanging.

10. Cut 5" x 11" rectangles from red fabric and fusible web; fuse together; do not remove paper backing. With stencils reversed, use pencil to draw around letters on paper side of fused rectangle; cut out. Position letters on background; fuse in place.

11. Leaving 5" streamers on each end, tie ribbon to buttons. Attach cards to ribbon with clothespins. Insert dowel through hanging sleeve.

PRIMITIVE SANTA
(Continued from page 34)

mustache, fold remaining ecru wool strip in half lengthwise and draw together with a stitch at center; glue beneath nose.

7. For hat, fold red wool circle in half. Referring to Fig. 1, fold again to form point of hat, glue in place. Use floss to sew a button to point of hat, knotting floss at front of button and leaving ¹/₂" tails.

Fig. 1

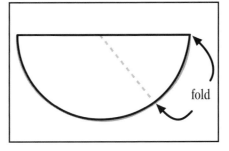
fold

8. Knotting ends at fronts of buttons, use floss to sew remaining buttons to front of Santa.

"NO PEEKIN'" DOOR HANGER
(Continued from page 23)

Fig. 2

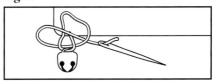

6. Spacing loops ¹/₂" apart and leaving floss slack between loops (Fig. 3), repeat Step 5 to add each remaining bell to pillow. Bring needle to back of pillow and secure floss.

Fig. 3

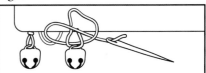

PATTERNS

SNOWMAN SWEATSHIRT

NOSE

SMILE

HAT

HATBAND

HEAD

ELF CHALKBOARD

KISS ME!!

MISTLETOE HAT

LARGE LEAVES

SMALL LEAVES

FESTIVE HOLIDAY MITTENS

SNOWMAN

TREE

TREE
TRUNK

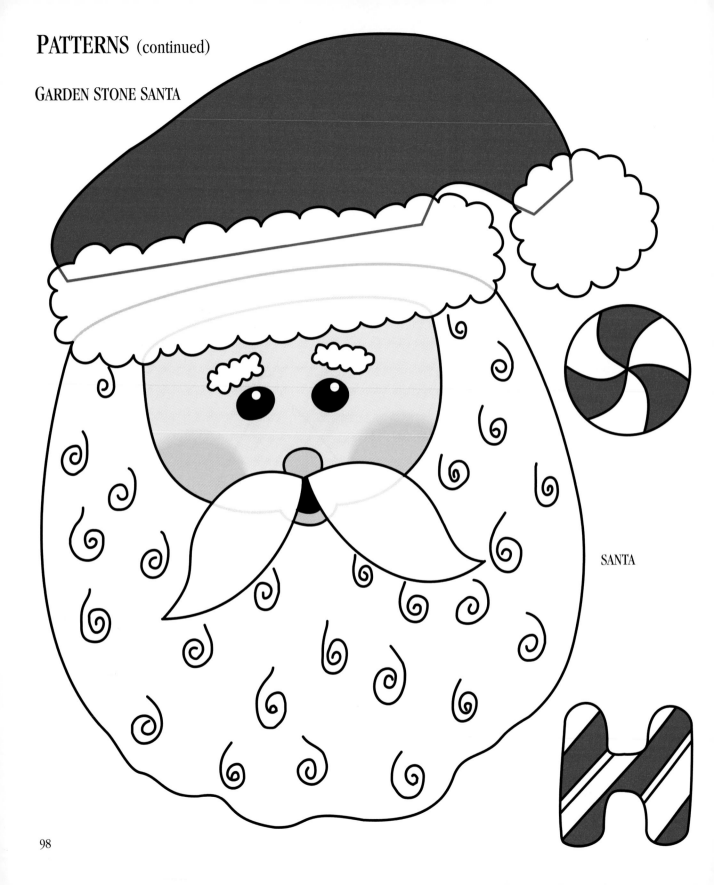

PATTERNS (continued)

GARDEN STONE SANTA

SANTA

FLOWER

FLOWER
CENTER

MITTEN

MITTEN CUFF

It's
Christmas
thyme

HEAD

CHRISTMAS KITCHEN ANGEL

PATTERNS (continued)

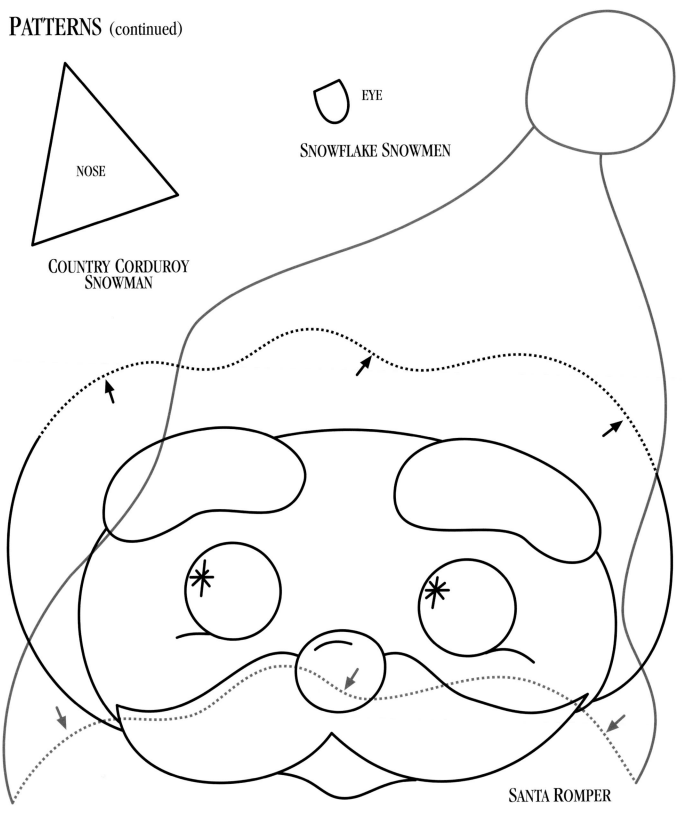

NOSE

COUNTRY CORDUROY SNOWMAN

EYE

SNOWFLAKE SNOWMEN

SANTA ROMPER

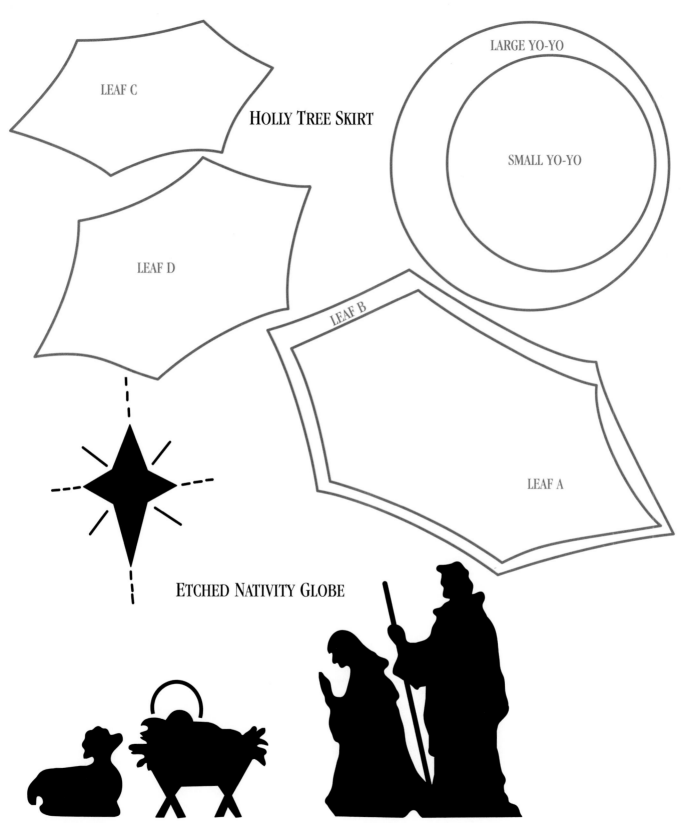

LEAF C

HOLLY TREE SKIRT

LARGE YO-YO

SMALL YO-YO

LEAF D

LEAF B

LEAF A

ETCHED NATIVITY GLOBE

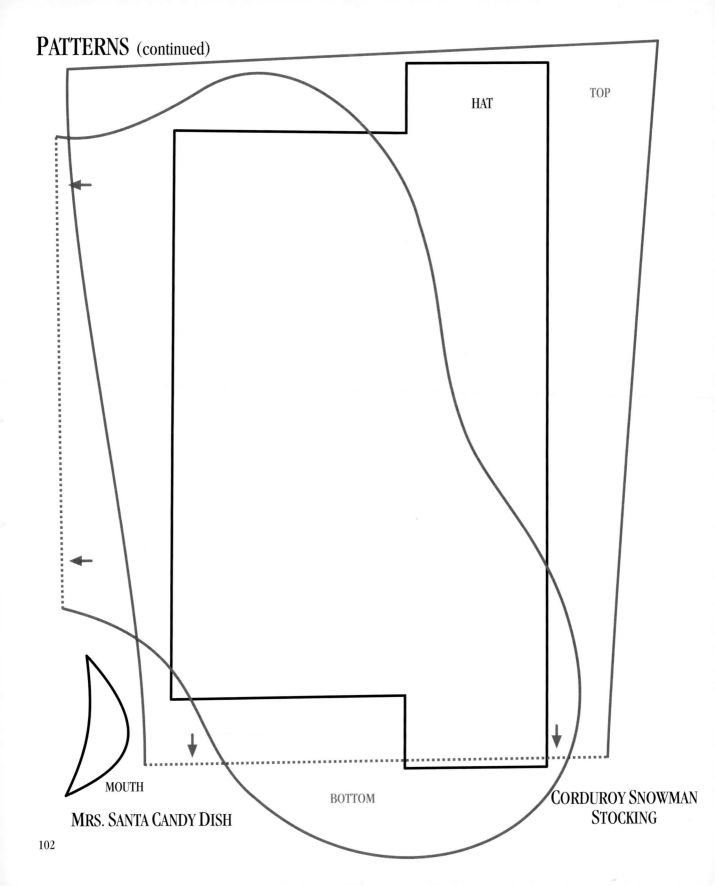

HAT

TOP

MOUTH

MRS. SANTA CANDY DISH

BOTTOM

CORDUROY SNOWMAN
STOCKING

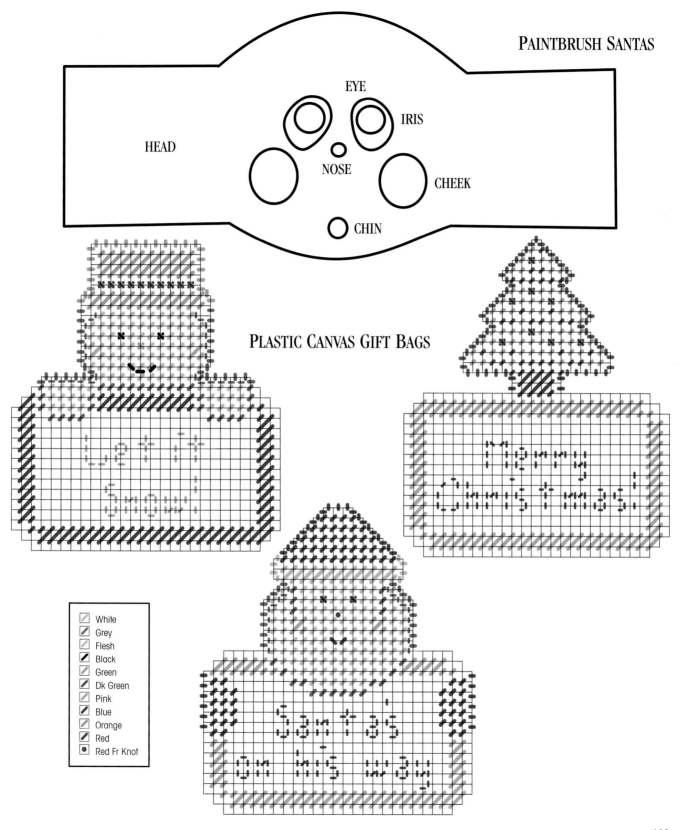

PAINTBRUSH SANTAS

EYE

IRIS

HEAD

NOSE

CHEEK

CHIN

PLASTIC CANVAS GIFT BAGS

▨	White
▨	Grey
▨	Flesh
◼	Black
▨	Green
◼	Dk Green
▨	Pink
◼	Blue
▨	Orange
◼	Red
⦿	Red Fr Knot

PATTERNS (continued)

HOLIDAY SWEATSHIRT

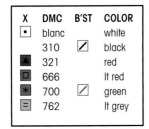

X	DMC	B'ST	COLOR
•	blanc		white
	310	/	black
▲	321		red
◻	666		lt red
✳	700	/	green
≡	762		lt grey

CROSS-STITCHED SNOWMEN STOCKING

X	DMC	¼X	B'ST	COLOR
•*	B5200	⊡		snow white
■*	310		/	black
◈	317			dk grey
◆	321			red
▲	334			blue
✳	413			vy dk grey
≡	415			lt grey
◆	433			lt brown
◻	666			lt red
◉	676			gold
+	677			lt gold
▲	729			dk gold
◉	762	◻		vy lt gold
★	910			dk green
	938		/*	dk brown
≡	912			green
✳	3713			pink
◻	3755			lt blue
◉	310			black Fr. Knot

* 3 skeins of B5200.
  2 skeins of 310.
  2 skeins of 938.

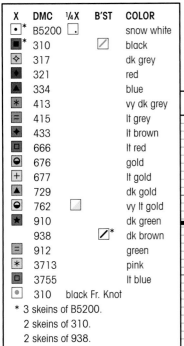

59w x 27h

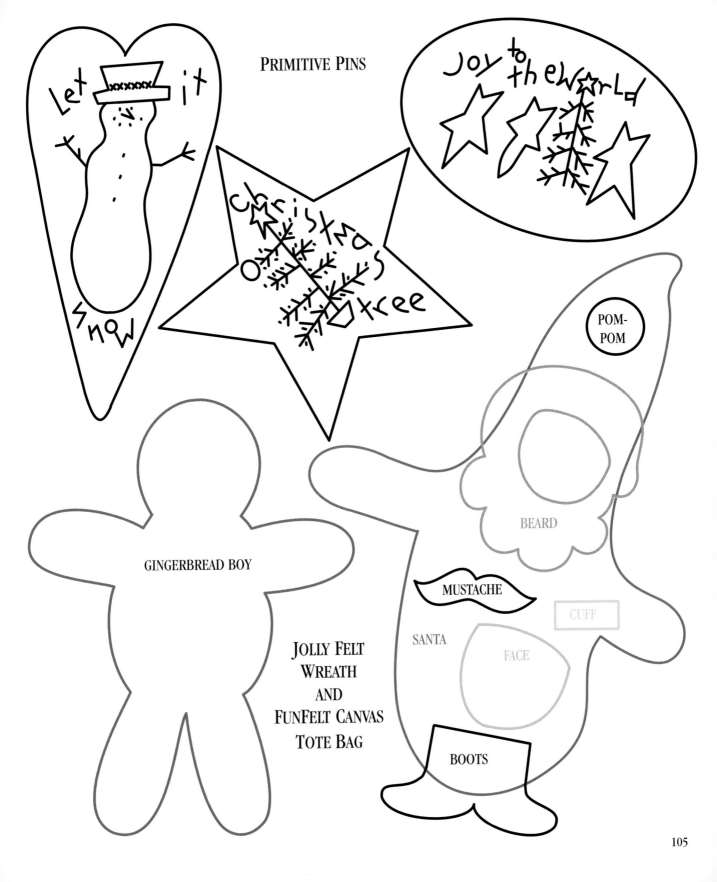

PRIMITIVE PINS

Let it snow

Joy to the world

christmas tree

GINGERBREAD BOY

POM-POM

BEARD

MUSTACHE

CUFF

SANTA

FACE

JOLLY FELT
WREATH
AND
FUNFELT CANVAS
TOTE BAG

BOOTS

PATTERNS (continued)

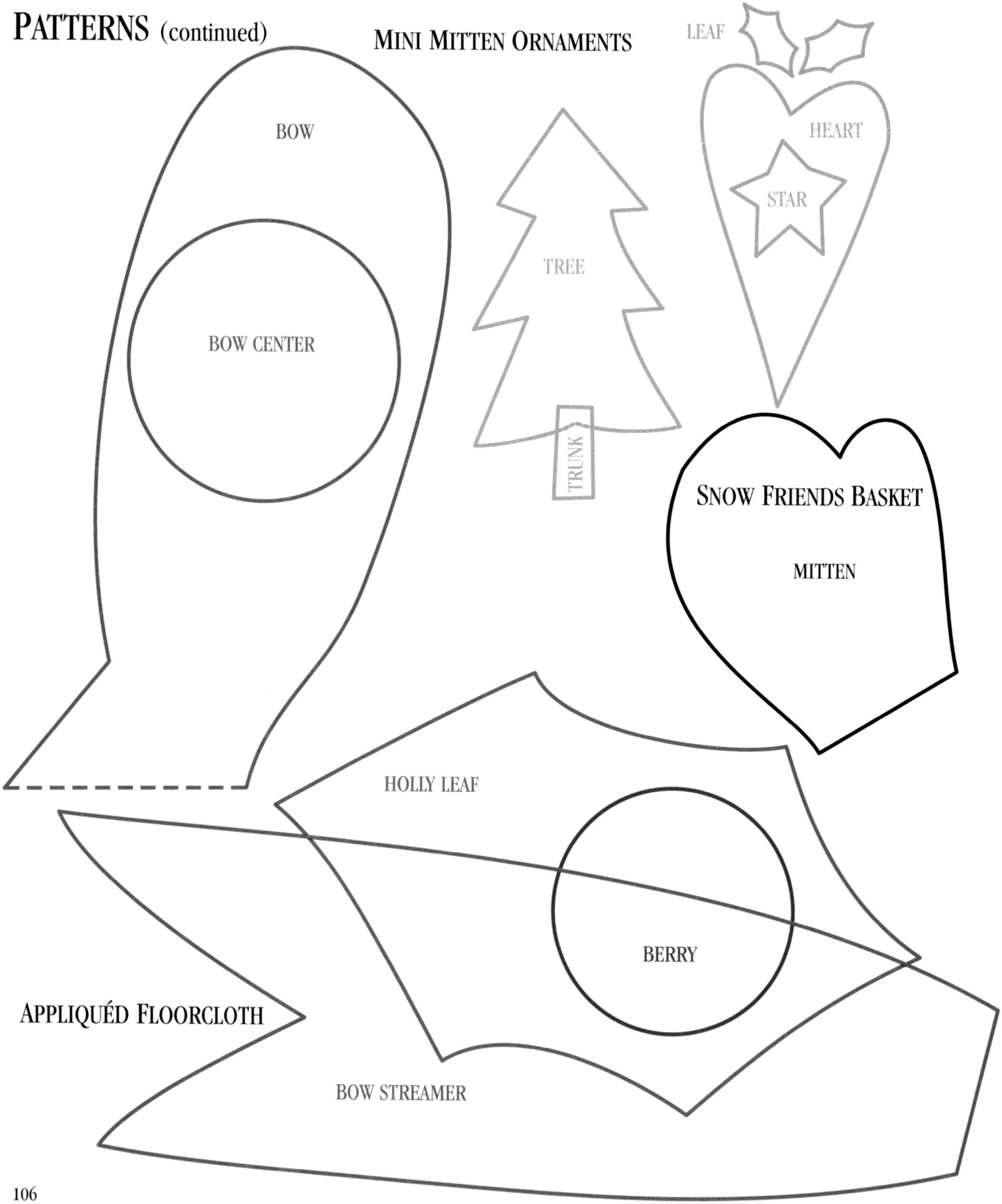

MINI MITTEN ORNAMENTS

LEAF

BOW

HEART

BOW CENTER

STAR

TREE

TRUNK

SNOW FRIENDS BASKET

MITTEN

HOLLY LEAF

BERRY

APPLIQUÉD FLOORCLOTH

BOW STREAMER

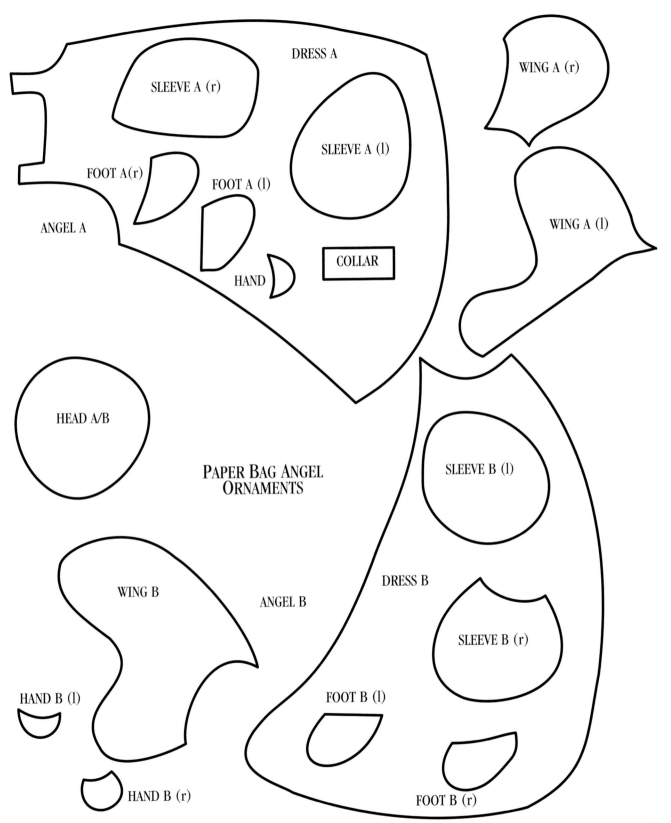

DRESS A

SLEEVE A (r)

WING A (r)

SLEEVE A (l)

FOOT A (r)

FOOT A (l)

WING A (l)

ANGEL A

HAND

COLLAR

HEAD A/B

SLEEVE B (l)

PAPER BAG ANGEL
ORNAMENTS

DRESS B

WING B

ANGEL B

SLEEVE B (r)

HAND B (l)

FOOT B (l)

HAND B (r)

FOOT B (r)

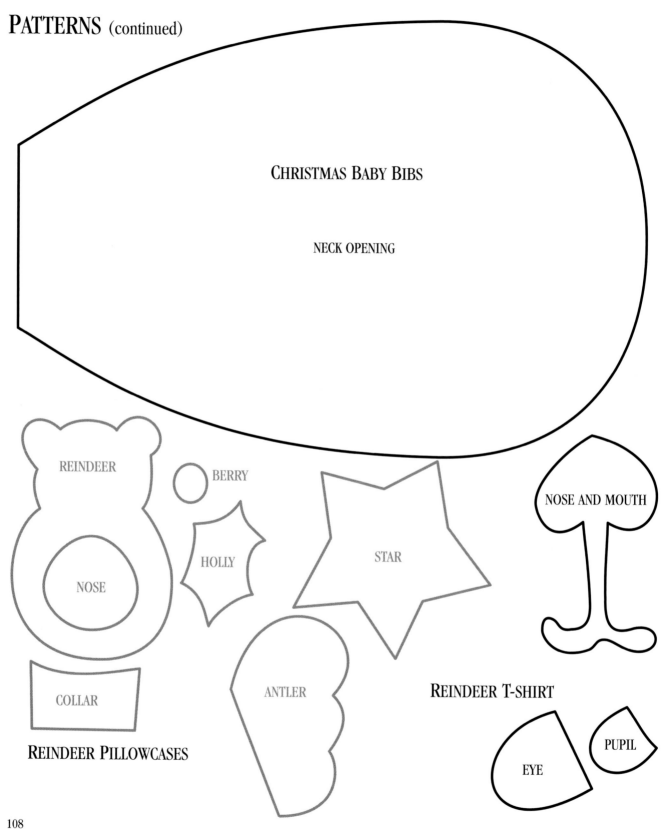

PATTERNS (continued)

CHRISTMAS BABY BIBS

NECK OPENING

REINDEER

BERRY

HOLLY

NOSE

STAR

NOSE AND MOUTH

COLLAR

ANTLER

REINDEER T-SHIRT

REINDEER PILLOWCASES

EYE

PUPIL

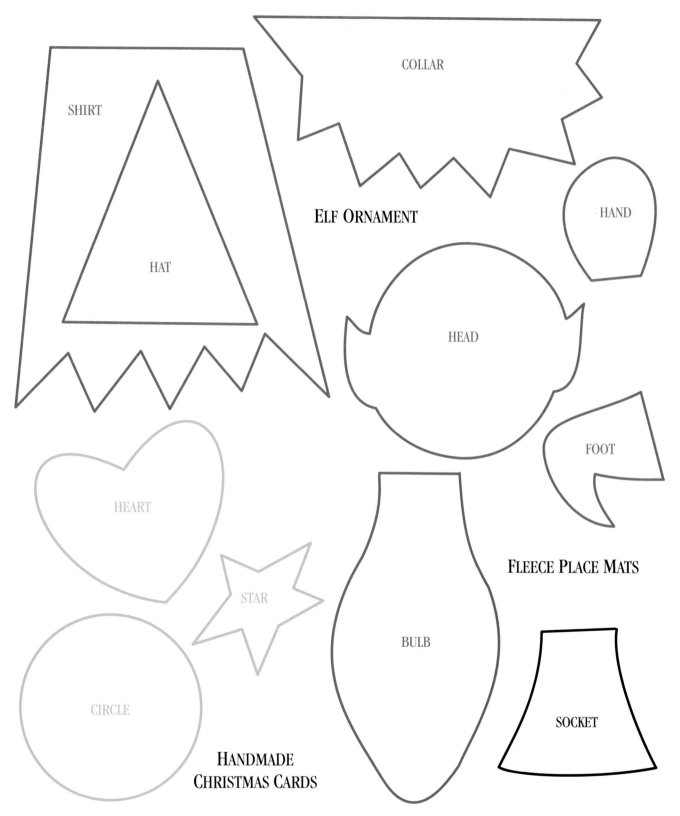

SHIRT

COLLAR

ELF ORNAMENT

HAT

HAND

HEAD

FOOT

HEART

FLEECE PLACE MATS

STAR

BULB

CIRCLE

SOCKET

HANDMADE
CHRISTMAS CARDS

PATTERNS (continued)

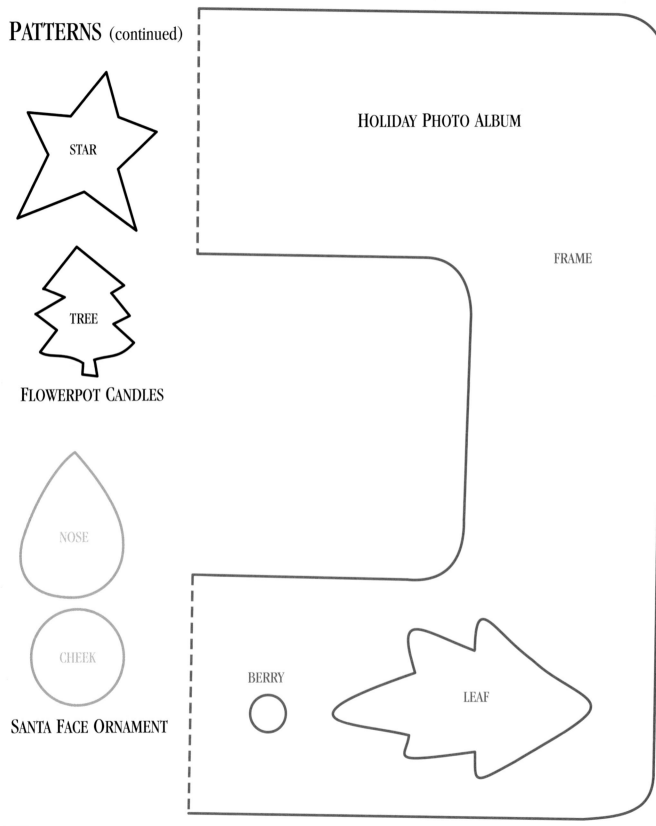

STAR

HOLIDAY PHOTO ALBUM

FRAME

TREE

FLOWERPOT CANDLES

NOSE

CHEEK

SANTA FACE ORNAMENT

BERRY

LEAF

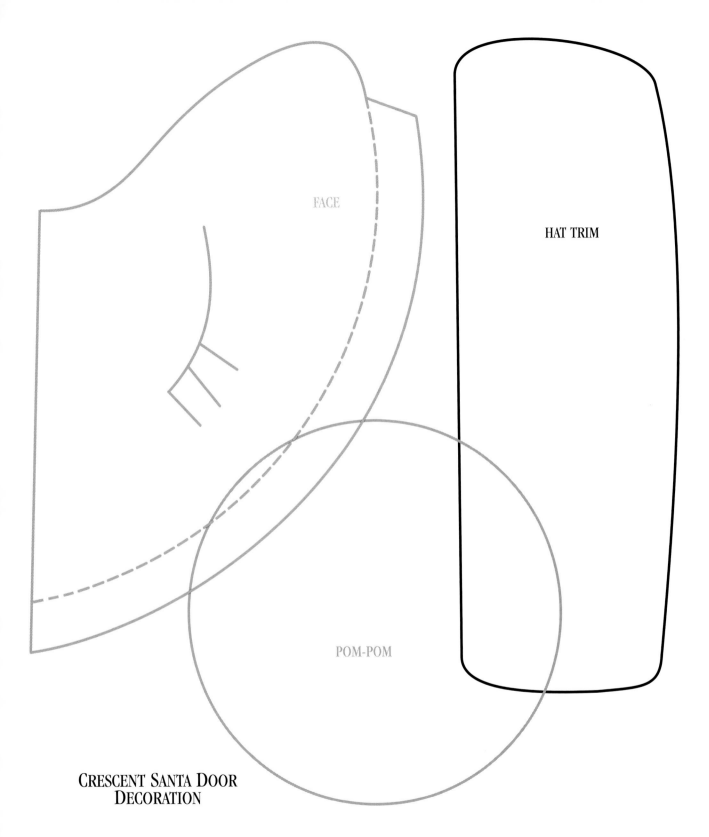

FACE

HAT TRIM

POM-POM

CRESCENT SANTA DOOR
DECORATION

111

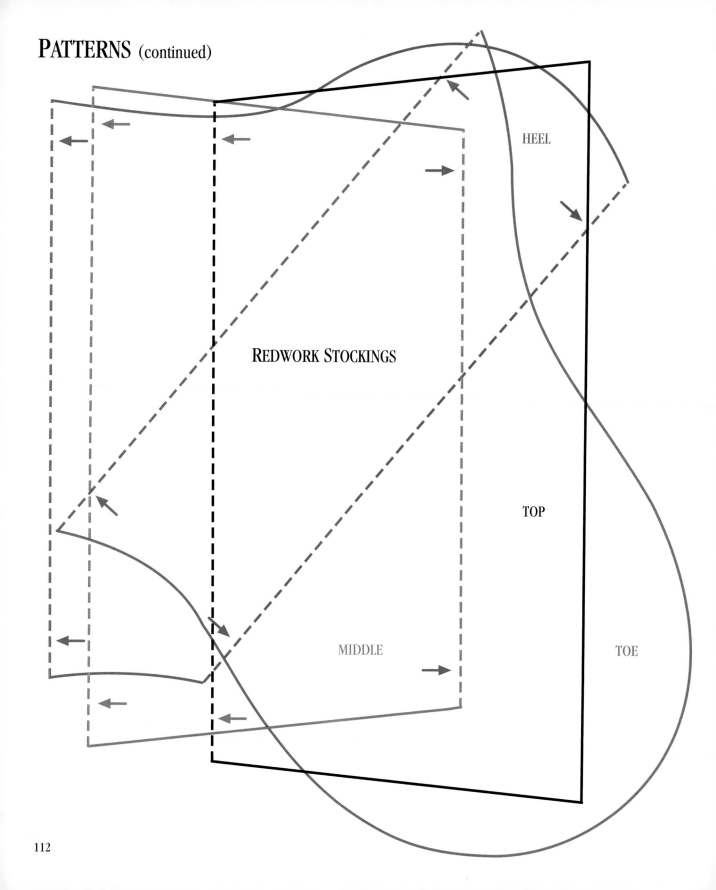

REDWORK STOCKINGS

HEEL

TOP

MIDDLE

TOE

MIDDLE

TOP

MERRY CHRISTMAS

REDWORK STOCKINGS
(continued)

TOE

LARGE HEART

SMALL HEART

LEAVES

HEART POCKET ORNAMENT

LEAF

"NO PEEKIN'" DOOR HANGER

114

It's Christmas!

time to trim the tree,
Wrap the Gifts, □
Bake the Cookies,
And Spend time
With Friends

PATTERNS (continued)

TREE

KIDS' PHOTO BOOKS

CHEEK

HEART

SNOWMAN

GINGERBREAD MAN

RUSTIC HOLIDAY WREATH

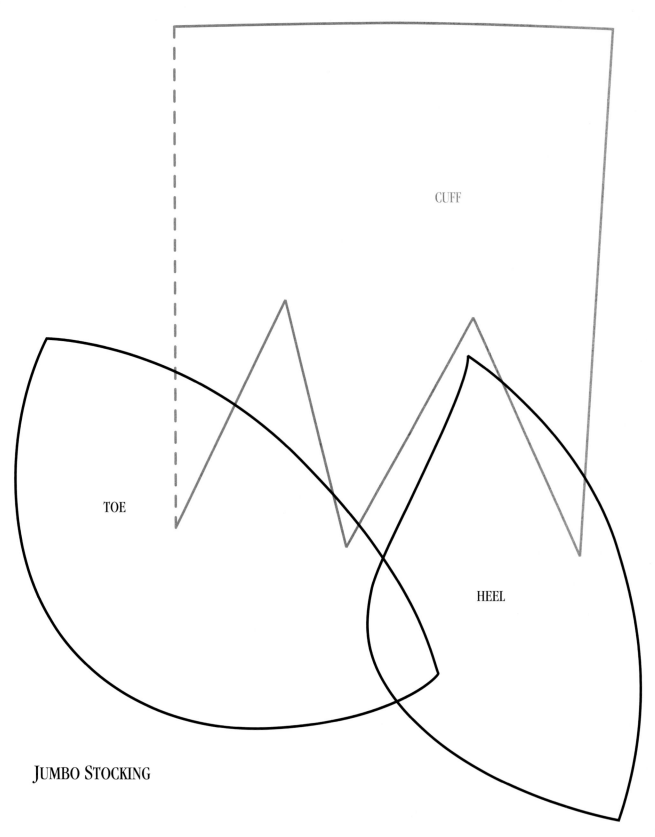

CUFF

TOE

HEEL

JUMBO STOCKING

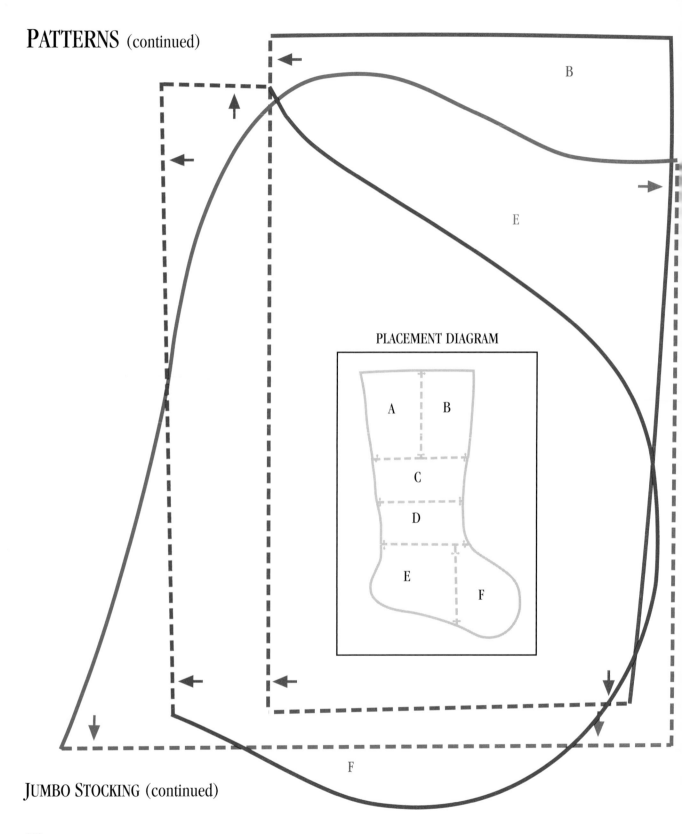

PLACEMENT DIAGRAM

A   B

C

D

E

F

B

E

F

JUMBO STOCKING (continued)

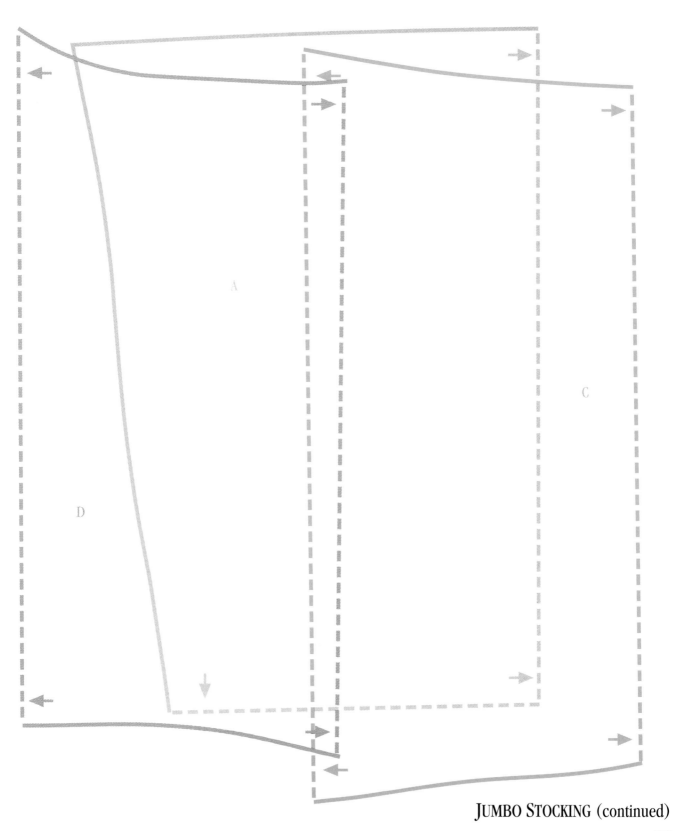

JUMBO STOCKING (continued)

HEAD

NOSE

HATBAND

HAT

FABRIC-COVERED BASKET

BERRY

LEAF

CHRISTMAS CARD
WALL HANGING

GINGERBREAD BOY

GOLD STAR WREATH

121

Making Patterns

Blue line on pattern indicates where traced pattern is to be placed on fold of fabric.

When patterns are stacked or overlapped, place tracing paper over pattern and follow a single colored line to trace pattern. Repeat to trace each pattern separately onto tracing paper.

For a more durable pattern, use translucent vinyl template material instead of tracing paper.

Half-patterns: Fold tracing paper in half. Place fold along dotted line and trace pattern half; turn folded paper over and draw over traced lines on remaining side. Unfold pattern; cut out.

Two-part patterns: Trace one part of pattern onto tracing paper. Match dotted line and arrows of traced part with dotted line and arrows of second part and trace second part; cut out.

Transferring a pattern: Make a tracing paper pattern. Position pattern on project. Place transfer paper coated side down between pattern and project. Use a stylus to trace over lines of patterns.

Making Appliqués

To protect your ironing board, cover with muslin. Web material that sticks to iron may be removed with hot iron cleaner, available at fabric and craft stores.

To prevent darker fabrics from showing through, white or light-colored fabrics may need to be lined with fusible interfacing before being used for appliqués.

Trace appliqué pattern onto paper side of web. If pattern is a half-pattern or to make a reversed appliqué, make a tracing paper pattern (turn traced pattern over for reversed appliqué) and follow instructions using traced pattern. When making more than one appliqué, leave at least 1" between shapes. Cutting $1/2$" outside drawn shape, cut out web shape. Fuse to wrong side of fabric. Cut out shape along drawn lines. Remove paper backing.

Stitching Appliqués

Place paper or stabilizer on wrong side of background fabric under fused or basted appliqué. Unless otherwise indicated in project instructions, use clear nylon thread and a narrow zigzag stitch.

Position project under presser foot so that most of stitching will be on appliqué. Take a stitch in fabric and bring bobbin thread to top. Hold both threads toward you and sew over them for several stitches to secure; clip threads. Stitch over all exposed raw edges of appliqué(s) and along detail lines as indicated in instructions.

When stitching is complete, remove stabilizer. Clip threads close to stitching.

Painting Basics

Painting with a sponge shape: Cut out sponge shape according to project instructions; dampen with water. Dip one side of sponge into paint and remove excess on a paper towel. Lightly press sponge shape on project, then carefully lift. Reapplying paint to sponge as necessary, repeat to paint additional shapes on project.

Sponge Painting: Pour a small amount of paint onto a paper plate. Dip dampened sponge piece into paint and remove excess on a paper towel. Use a light stamping motion to apply paint. Reapply paint to sponge as necessary.

Sealing: If an item will be handled frequently or used outdoors, we recommend sealing the item with a clear acrylic sealer. Sealers are available in spray or brush-on form in several finishes. Follow manufacturer's instructions to apply sealer.

Painting with dimensional paint: Turn bottle upside down to fill tip before each use. While painting, clean tip often with a paper towel. If tip becomes clogged, insert a straight pin into opening to unclog.

To paint, touch tip to project. Squeezing and moving bottle steadily, apply paint to project, being careful not to flatten paint line. If painting detail lines, center line of paint over transferred line on project or freehand details as desired.

To correct a mistake, use a paring knife to gently scrape excess paint from project before it dries. Carefully remove stain with non-acetone nail polish remover on a cotton swab. A mistake may also be camouflaged by incorporating it into the design.

MAKING A POM-POM

Cut a 3" square of cardboard. Wind yarn around cardboard about 100 times. Carefully slip the yarn off the cardboard and firmly knot an 18" length of yarn around middle. Leave yarn ends long enough to attach pom-pom to project. Cut loops and trim to shape pom-pom into a smooth ball. Fluff pom-pom by rolling between hands. Use long yarn ends to attach pom-pom to project.

MAKING POURED CANDLES

Caution: Do not melt wax over an open flame or in a pan placed directly on burner.

1. Cover work area with newspaper.

2. Fill a large saucepan with 1" of water. Heat water to boiling; reduce heat to simmer.

3. Place wax in a large can. If pouring wax, pinch rim of can to form a spout.

4. Place can in simmering water. Add additional water to pan as necessary. As wax melts, stir occasionally with craft stick.

5. Cut a length of wax-coated wick 1" longer than depth of mold or container.

6. Using an oven mitt, carefully pour wax into mold or container.

7. Allow wax to harden slightly; insert wick into candle. Allow wax to harden completely.

8. As wax hardens, a depression may form in candle surface. If desired, melt additional wax and add enough to fill depression.

MAKING A BOW

For first streamer, measure length of desired streamer from one end of ribbon and twist ribbon between fingers.

For first loop, keep right side of ribbon facing out and fold ribbon to form desired size loop; gather between fingers.

Fold ribbon to back to form another loop; gather between fingers. Continue to form loops until bow is desired size.

For remaining streamer, trim ribbon to desired length.

To secure bow, hold gathered loops tightly. Fold a length of floral wire around gathers. Holding wire ends behind bow and gathering loops forward; twist bow to tighten wire. Arrange loops and trim ribbon ends as desired.

CUTTING A FABRIC CIRCLE

Matching right sides, fold fabric square in half from top to bottom and in half again from left to right.

Refer to project instructions for diameter of fabric circle; determine radius of circle by dividing diameter in half. Tie one end of string to fabric marking pencil. Insert thumbtack through fabric as shown in Fig. 1; mark cutting line. Cut along drawn line through all fabric layers. Unfold circle.

Fig. 1

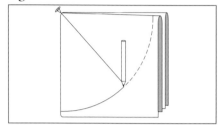

COVERING A LAMPSHADE

1. To make pattern, find seamline of lampshade. If shade does not have a seamline, draw a vertical line from top edge to bottom edge of shade.

2. Center tissue paper edge on shade seamline; tape in place. Wrap paper around shade extending one inch past seamline; tape to secure (Fig. 1).

Fig. 1

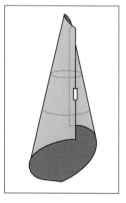

3. Trace along top and bottom edges of shade. Draw a vertical line from top edge to bottom edge of shade 1" past seamline. Remove paper; cut along drawn lines.

4. Use pattern to cut cover from desired fabric or paper.

5. Fold one straight edge of covering ½" to wrong side; press.

6. Matching unpressed straight edge of covering to seamline, use spray adhesive to apply covering to shade. Use craft glue to secure pressed edge.

EMBROIDERY STITCHES

Preparing floss: If using embroidery floss for a project that will be laundered, soak floss in a mixture of one cup water and one tablespoon vinegar for a few minutes and allow to dry before using to prevent colors from bleeding or fading.

Backstitch: Referring to Fig. 1, come up at 1 and go down at 2; bring up at 3 and pull through. For next stitch, insert needle at 1; bring up at 4 and pull through.

Fig. 1

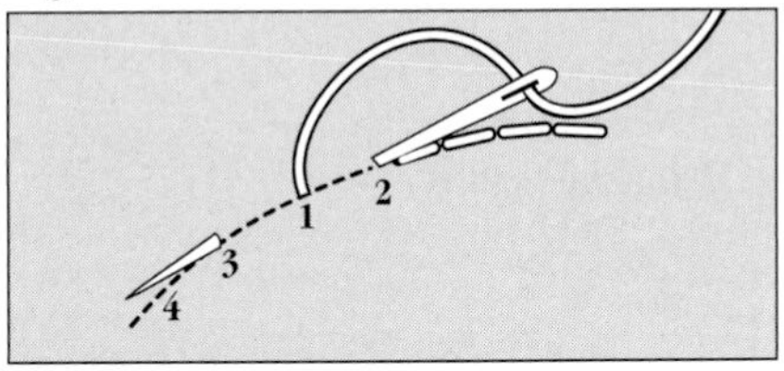

Blanket Stitch: Referring to Fig. 2, bring needle up at 1. Keeping thread below point of needle, go down at 2 and come up at 3. Continue working as shown in Fig. 3.

Fig. 2

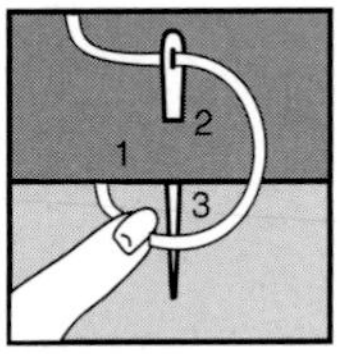

Fig. 3

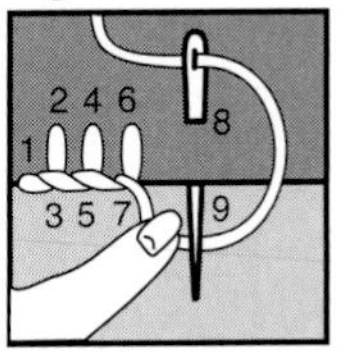

Couching Stitch: Thread first needle with desired number of strands of floss to be couched. Thread a second needle with stitching floss. Bring first needle up through fabric. Using second needle, bring needle up at 1 and down at 2 to secure floss (Fig. 4). Repeat to secure floss along desired line.

Fig. 4

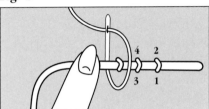

Cross Stitch: Referring to Fig. 5, bring needle up at 1; go down at 2. Bring needle up at 3; go down at 4. Repeat for each stitch.

Fig. 5

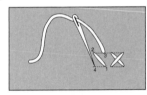

French Knot: Referring to Fig. 6, bring needle up at 1. Wrap floss once around needle and insert needle at 2, holding end of floss with non-stitching fingers. Tighten knot, then pull needle through fabric, holding floss until it must be released. For a larger knot, use more strands; wrap only once.

Fig. 6

Lazy Daisy Stitch: Referring to Fig. 7, come up at 1 and make a loop with the thread. Go back down at 1 and come up at 2, keeping the thread below point of needle. Secure loop by bringing thread over loop and going down at 2.

Fig. 7

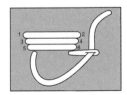

Running Stitch: Referring to Fig. 8, make a series of straight stitches with stitch length equal to the space between stitches.

Fig. 8

Satin Stitch: Referring to Fig. 9, come up at odd numbers and go down at even numbers with the stitches touching but not overlapping.

Fig. 9

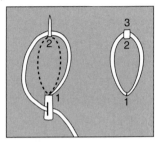

Stem Stitch: Referring to Fig. 10, come up at 1. Keeping the thread below the stitching line, go down at 2 and come up at 3. Go down at 4 and come up at 5.

Fig. 10

Straight Stitch: Referring to Fig. 11, come up at 1 and go down at 2.

Fig. 11

PLASTIC CANVAS

Gobelin Stitch: Referring to Fig. 1, work stitch over 2 or more threads or intersections. The number of threads or intersections may vary according to the chart.

Fig. 1

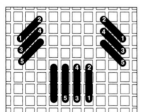

Backstitch: Referring to Fig. 2, work stitch over completed stitches to outline or define. It is sometimes worked over more than one thread. Backstitch may also be used to cover canvas.

Fig. 2

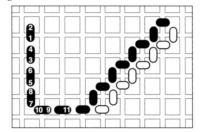

Cross Stitch: This stitch is composed of two stitches. The top of each cross must always be made in the same direction (Fig. 3).

Fig. 3

French Knot: Referring to Fig. 4, bring needle up through hole; wrap yarn once around needle and insert needle in same hole, holding end of yarn with non-stitching fingers. Tighten knot, then pull needle through canvas, holding yarn until it must be released.

Fig. 4

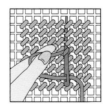

Overcast Stitch: This stitch covers the edge of the plastic canvas and joins pieces of canvas. It may be necessary to go through the same hole more than once to get even coverage on the edge, especially at the corners (Fig. 5).

Fig. 5

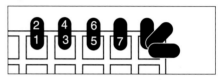

Tent Stitch: Referring to Fig. 6, work stitch in vertical or horizontal rows over one intersection.

Fig. 6

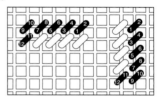

Mosiac Stitch: This three-stitch pattern forms small squares (Fig. 7).

Fig. 7

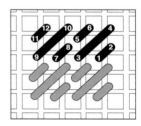

CROSS STITCH

Preparing floss: If using emroidery floss for a project that will be laundered, soak floss in a mixture of one cup water and one tablespoon vinegar for a few minutes and allow to dry before using to prevent colors from bleeding or fading.

Working on Waste Canvas: Cut pieces of waste canvas and lightweight interfacing about 1" larger on all sides than finished design size. Center and pin interfacing to inside front of garment. Cover edges of canvas with masking tape. Find center of stitching area on canvas and mark with a pin. Find center of stitching area on garment and mark with a pin. Matching center of canvas to pin on garment, pin canvas in place. Stitching through all layers, baste along edges of canvas, from corner to corner, and from side to side. Mark center of canvas by using contrasting thread to baste down center. Beginning 1" from top of canvas, use a sharp needle to stitch design. Remove basting threads and trim canvas to about ¹/₂" from design. Use tweezers to pull out canvas threads one at a time. If necessary, dampen canvas until it becomes soft enough to make removing threads easier.

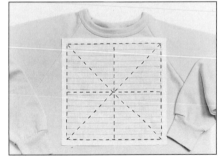

Counted Cross Stitch (X): Work one Cross Stitch to correspond to each colored square in chart. For horizontal rows, work stitches in two journeys.

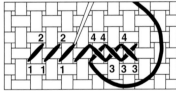

For vertical rows, complete each stitch as shown.

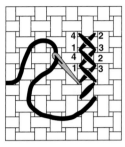

Quarter Stitch (¹/₄ X): Quarter Stitches are shown by triangular shapes of color in chart and color key.

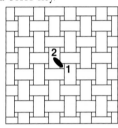

Backstitch (B'ST): For outline detail, Backstitch (shown in chart and color key by black or colored straight lines) should be worked after all Cross Stitch has been completed.

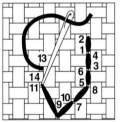

CROCHET
Abbreviations:

ch(s)	chain(s)
dc	double crochet(s)
mm	millimeters
Rnd(s)	Round(s)
sc	single crochet(s)
st(s)	stitch(es)
YO	yarn over

★ — work instructions following ★ as many more times as indicated in addition to the first time.

† to † — work all instructions from first † to second † as many times as specified.

( ) — work enclosed instructions as many times as specified by the number immediately following or work all enclosed instructions in the stitch or space indicated or contains explanatory remarks.

Gauge: Gauge is the number of stitches and rows or rounds per inch and is used to make sure your project will be the correct size. The hook size given in the instructions is just a guide. The project should never be made without first making a sample swatch about 4" square using the thread or yarn, hook, and stitch specified. Measure the swatch, counting stitches and rows carefully. If your swatch is smaller than what is specified in the instructions, try again with a larger hook; if it's larger, try again with a smaller one. Keep trying until you find the size hook that will give you the specified gauge.

Single crochet (sc): Insert hook in stitch or space indicated, YO and pull up a loop, YO and draw through both loops on hook.

Double crochet (dc): YO, insert hook in stitch or space indicated, YO and pull up a loop, YO and draw through 2 loops on hook. YO and draw though remaining 2 loops on hook.

Back loops only (BLO): When instructed to work in back loops only, work in loops indicated by arrow.

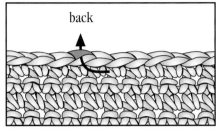

Free loops of a chain: When instructed to work in free loops of a chain, work in loop indicated by arrow.

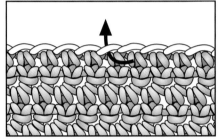

Joining with sc: When instructed to join with sc, begin with a slip knot on hook. Insert hook in specified stitch or space and pull up a loop, YO and draw through both loops on hook.

Changing colors: To change colors, work last sc before color change to last step (2 loops on hook), with new color, YO and pull through; drop old color.

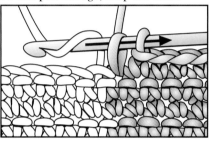

Finishing hints: Good finishing techniques make a big difference in the quality of the finished piece. Make a habit of weaving in loose ends as you work. To keep loose ends from showing, always weave them back through several stitches or work over them. When ends are secure, clip them off close to work.

CREDITS

We want to extend a warm *thank you* to the generous people who allowed us to photograph our projects at their homes: Joan Adams, Charlie and Peg Mills, Julie Mullins, Duncan and Nancy Porter, and Leighton Weeks.

To Magna IV Color Imaging of Little Rock, Arkansas, we say *thank you* for the superb color reproduction and excellent pre-press preparation.

We want to especially thank photographers Larry Pennington, Mark Mathews, and Ken West of Peerless Photography, Little Rock, Arkansas, for their time, patience, and excellent work.

To the talented people who helped in the creation of the following projects in this book, we extend a special word of thanks:

- *Cross-Stitched Snowmen Stocking*, page 21: Deborah A. Lambein
- *Crocheted Stocking,* page 43: Maggie Weldon
- *Holiday Sweatshirt* cross-stitch design, page 63: Vicki Howard
- *Plastic Canvas Gift Bags,* page 68: Ann Townsend

Thanks also go to the people who assisted in making and testing projects in this book: Connie McGaughey, Judy Shirley, and Judy Simmons.